Receiving Answers and
Words of Wisdom

Receiving Answers and Words of Wisdom

Jan Tyler Bray

Stellium Flame

Published in 2019 by Stellium Flame, Plymouth UK

www.stelliumpub.com

Copyright © 2019 by the author, Jan Tyler Bray,
who has asserted her moral right
to be identified as the author of this work
in accordance with sections 77 & 78 of
The Copyright, Designs and Patents Act 1988

A CIP record for this book is available from the British Library

Cover illustration by Andrew Naumann, copyright © 2019

ISBN: 978-1-912358-05-2

About the Author

After Jan lost her father in 2004, she started an intensive search to try and contact him; she felt that he was still near her somehow, and she joined spiritualist circles and groups, learning to meditate and to communicate with the other side.

In time, Jan's contacts developed to the extent that her Guide would pass wisdom across to her, with the intention that this information should be spread widely, to help people with spiritual and other kinds of needs.

Contents

Receiving Answers and Words of Wisdom

Introduction

If you were kind enough to read my first book you will know that when I lost my Dad, I felt a great need to try to find out where he had gone, on losing my Mum my search deepened. Over a period of fourteen years or so, I have been privileged to meet my Guide, Father Benedict, who is a 12th century Benedictine monk and lives on Lindisfarne Island in the north of England. He gives me little teachings through inspired writing, so I may pass them on to others to help them to understand their loss and the world around them. Sometimes I have a question, and other times I am given messages of philosophy to help people lead more peaceful and contented lives.

As a side note when I first began channelling information, I understood that I must not change any of the words I received, which I didn't in my first book, but I now realise that obviously whilst the content must remain true, it's quite all right for me to change the grammar.

There is Nothing New in the World

Anything you may be experiencing is only the same thing that has occurred over and over before in history, and indeed to you also, any solution will be the same, the answers will be no different no matter what time frame you happen to be in, but each time your upsets and problems arise they will have a slightly different twist to them. If you feel as you read through this book you have read or heard these things before, you will be right because there is nothing new to deal with, the difference is, it will be presented in a slightly alternative way as to resonate with everyone on their own vibration and way of processing events. It has been said before to take what fits and reject for now what doesn't, because you cannot have harmony and understanding if you don't feel it in your soul. Realistically no life is ever smooth running all the time, but you may think to yourself mine seems to stack up a lot higher than most, and you will definitely know that person who's life appears to be perfect, perfect partner, perfect body, perfect kids, perfect home etc, but do not delude yourself for no matter how you view it, and wish it were yours, each life comes with its own set of problems and tasks to be completed by that person, their tasks will definitely be different to yours, and that's what will be blinding you. You will look at your life and compare it to theirs, some of which they will have either completed in previous lifetimes or are yet to come, but to your eyes they do not have a problem. Some will have unsuccessful relationships, some money problems, some health issues and whatever ails each person will be different to yours, but you will only see the ones you have chosen to experience this time around. Each time you do come across bumps in the road or long-term delays try your best to understand the reasons behind what's causing them and try to deal with them with a positive mind and attitude.

Talking to Spirit

It's a sad reality that most people only talk to spirit when they are in need. It's strange but if you were to ask the majority if they believe in heaven, or the afterlife most would be sitting on the fence, they don't like to commit themselves by stating, "yes I do believe," because they like to have evidence, but it is also true that once they find themselves in sticky, upsetting or frightening situations they unconsciously begin talking to....? who is it they are pleading with to make it right, and if you think about it, why should whoever it is listen when things are going bad, because when things are going great and they would like to share in them, they never get an invitation. How many people remember to say thank you for this lovely day, sunrise, safe journey, food on my plate etc, and the answer is, not many and that's sad. Pleaded with in the bad times and ignored in the good, a change is needed, if for no other reason to share in the good times the bond becomes stronger, so when you do need help your voice is recognised, because spirit could be confused and think who is that talking to me? Or, I do know who you are? You're the one complaining about how bad your life is. Be recognised for being a happy, appreciative person who's having a great life, because by now most of you understand that like attracts like, which means for everything that you're acknowledging and thanking for, you will attract more of the same to you, and for everything that you're complaining about, you will attract more to complain about. So, if you haven't already gotten into the habit of talking to spirit, thanking for the good as well as asking for help with the bad, then please make a start today.

Thank-you Father Benedict.

3

Time Is an Illusion

Once again, I find myself flying over the sea to the Island, it's a lot like the opening credits to a TV program, I'm above all observing, I circle around and see the Fathers working in their vegetable garden, its Spring and a time for planting and preparing.

Father Benedict Speaks to Me
Everything has a time of its own, and everything happens in just the order it's meant to. Sometimes it feels as though the plants take so long before the little green shoots begin to appear, and at other times no sooner have you planted them, then up they pop. Some hours feel like days, some days feel like weeks, and you think is this just fantasy thinking on my part, time is time and it can't change but it can, time can be stretched out or slowed down, it's all in the hands of the perceiver. Time is an illusion and can be bent into different curves, and shapes to suit purpose or activity. When you are engrossed in something pleasurable, time seems to fly by in a moment and this is actually the case, you speed up the time, the vibrations that surround the activity will pulsate at a faster frequency, and because of the nature of the high vibrations, they will knock against each other and join as one, instead of being separate. As the two join others will also, there by speeding up time itself, anything that's thoroughly enjoyed, appreciated and loved will carry forward at a greater speed. It's the same in reverse when it's applied to something you don't particularly like, time will literally drag by. The molecules and atoms will split into ever smaller ones, because of the negative vibrations that are carried within; they break apart, there by stretching out time itself, making the unpleasant activity seem endless. So, is time an illusion? Yes, it is. When people say you can make time for anything, you can if you really want to, do not find yourself rushing around, trying to accomplish everything and gaining nothing, for the more you rush the more time will elude you. Pace yourself and take time to attend to things properly, take a pride in what you do, and always give it your best shot, for when you do this, instead of

4

just getting things out of the way as fast as you can, you will achieve more in less time, and feel fulfilled and content with what you've done.

Thank-you Father Benedict.

Think of Others before it's Too Late

(Atlantis)

For the second time Father Benedict and I walk into the sea, I find it cold as we begin, but within a short time I get used to the feeling. We walk together into the small waves at the shore, and then further out until we are walking underneath them altogether, it feels as though we are flying, we are weightless, we are floating, and yet strangely it feels perfectly normal to be doing this. We walk, and as we do it feels like we are walking back through time and space, I see in the distance great buildings with pillars, the whole scene is very large and regal and reminds me of ancient Greece. We are under the sea but we're breathing air, it's all very surreal, I look around and see people at their daily tasks, I'm an observer but also part of it. What at first appears to be scenes of harmony on closer inspection, I can feel undercurrents of discord, and there is tension and fear, fear of scarcity. There is beauty and abundance everywhere and the city is very affluent, but still I sense poverty, not quite everyone but certainly most people, appear to be self-absorbed and somewhat greedy, wanting all and sharing nothing, without much thought for others. They seem vain and self-centred, caring far too much about their own appearance, to the point of obsession. The karmic debt is gathering and gaining strength, and the cause of all these selfish actions will soon be felt as an effect in the lifestyle, and in life itself. People are so interested in the lives of others, not unlike the drama on television shows, gossiping, stirring up trouble, telling lies, and making up wild stories to impress each other, the undercurrent is heavy and jaded. There are a few here, who try to teach love and compassion, but they are being swallowed up by the majority, gossip is not helpful because it produces negative vibrations which will increase with time. The air is thick and suffocating, at first glance it looks like a pleasant place to live, wide open spaces with beautiful buildings, luxury is everywhere, gold and jewels are abundant, and on the face of it every soul should be content and happy, but look a little closer, those smiles are superficially painted in place, they're false just like many other things about their bodies, they're unnatural, they may look perfect but as with most things here, there seems to be an agenda to it all. My head is in a whirl, Father Benedict lets me watch for a while longer, then pulls me to one side and we walk back to our shoreline in silence. I need to regain my calm because I'm feeling anxious and upset, he explains to me that although there are many people on the earth today who are genuinely concerned about the welfare of others, the care and preservation of the planet, and positive thoughts of love for their fellow man but there are still many more who are obsessed about themselves, their looks and their trappings of life, they have painted on faces and they love to gossip and make trouble, all these things need to be addressed and life should become simple again, there needs to be more concern and love, compassion and happiness, because if the negative vibrations overtake the positive ones, then I'm afraid there will be another Atlantis, I now understand what he was showing me under the waves. He tells me life will be swallowed up by itself, it will be as the snake who starts to eat its own tail, there is no awareness to the consequences of its actions, so it carries on regardless until it has eaten itself, and there is nothing left at all. So please forget the gossip the greed, the silly self- obsession and spread the love, for this is the only way to move forward and keep this beautiful planet alive.

Thank-you Father Benedict.

Hand Things Over

I walk across the causeway at low tide and I see Father Benedict waiting for me, I find myself running towards him and I give him a big hug, he hugs me back smiles, and says welcome you are happy today, exciting times to come for you. We then walk along the shoreline, it's lovely and warm, just the sort of weather I like.

Father Benedict Speaks to Me

After the storm comes the calm, the contentment and the peace. I see there is a change in you and that is good because you as everyone must learn to stop the struggle within your heart and your head. All beings seem to feel it's their job to be able to "fix" everything that comes their way, they struggle, push themselves into tight corners and wear themselves out, both physically and mentally and all because they are conditioned to do so. We'd love to shout stop! Stop the struggle and the torment, you cannot fix all things and you shouldn't even try. Let it go and hand things over to the universe, as it can see much clearer what's required. We get upset and frustrated, but because we are governed by universal laws, that state we can do nothing until you set your burdens down and verbally hand things over to us, we too are stuck. We will of course not take away lessons, for they are yours, but we will upon request fan out in all directions to help you to sort things out, we will present people who are just what you will need to get the job done, we'll open up situations and places needed, to enable you to keep your energies and vibrations high and clear, we will put that smile back on your face, and love in your heart, so in this happy place it will seem that as if by magic your life has turned a corner.

Life is only a problem if you let it be, when you let all those little things build up into something far too big, you may find yourself stuck repeating the same pattern over and over and sometimes for years, but as we've said before time really has no meaning at all, in earth years a pattern of health or relationship issues, can keep going around and around for a very long time, but in reality it doesn't matter if its left until five minutes to twelve, (midnight being the end of an earth life) as long as it is sorted out, peace will then prevail. Speak to us often because we can help you more than you could ever know, but we do need your voice because it's the vibration that is uniquely yours that each soul will recognise, it's a bit like belonging to an elite group or club, where the members have a secret pass word, or symbol the others share. Realise that both sides of the glass, the "living" and the "dead" are divided into large family groups, that care very deeply about each other, and will do all within their power to help you have a great life, but you do need to ask first.

Thank-you Father Benedict.

I Have a Question

Question: Why do guides often appear as Native Americans, Ethnic groups, or Religious people?

Answer: For some people who are still sitting on the fence about things spiritual, they puzzle about the fact that Guides and helpers seem to be as you have asked, and it appears to them to be a bit of a cliché. The answer is of course that once people have passed over, they don't really change that much, so if the knowledge wasn't that extensive up to the point of passing, you won't have such a great wealth of information to pass on, where-as the groups of people you have asked about, would have understood how the natural laws of the universe and nature work, because they would have lived by them. Guides and helpers don't have a form as such, because when you return home the physical form is obviously of no use now, and when you reincarnate your form will be different every time, but because earth bodies recognise the physical body and not necessarily the energy body, your Guides will chose to portray themselves as they have incarnated at some time, for example a religious or indigenous person, because when in this state they will have lived a life closer to nature, only used what was needed and not wasted anything or took things for granted, they would have been thankful and bless all that came their way. They understood the seasons and the importance of eating seasonally, fishing or hunting what was abundant at that time, in the winter when there wasn't a lot around, they would have rested more, animals hibernate to conserve their energies and the humans would have done the same, because there wouldn't have been much to sustain their energy levels. Of course, there were no electric lights so when darkness came it meant time to sleep, in the summer when the days were long, and food was abundant for their fuel they would have worked and played hard and had enough food and sunlight to recharge their batteries. There is a natural order to all things, and to live in this way, is to be in harmony and at peace with the world and oneself. Today you can have anything you want to eat at any time, but foods that are eaten out of season will not do a body as good as those that are in season, because of the natural energies contained within the food itself, bodies require different energies at different times of the year. It's the same with sleep and rest, winter is the time for rest and summer the time for activity, more babies are conceived in the winter, so once the spring and summer comes around the new infant will benefit from warm sunny days, and plentiful supplies of food via the Mother and what she has eaten.

So, although your Guides and helpers may show themselves to you as particular sets of people the real reason they are Guides, is they've They've had more lifetimes and gained more knowledge through experience than others.

Thank-you Father Benedict.

It's Wrong to Hate

Not just from a moral point of view but from a practical one also. Hatred does not cease by loathing, only through love will it end. When someone has hurt you, your loved ones or family, you may think it's only natural to hate them, but by giving away your precious energy you will be keeping that hurt alive. Hate is not a normal reaction for the soul to have, it is distorted thinking and it's harmful for your health, it is the ego at its best, it's confusion and it's a conflict of idea's and value's. Everyone feels they are right and will probably be trying to get their friends and family on side, by saying what a bad person the other is, and in most cases that "bad" person will be doing the same, trying to justify their actions. Everyone is on their own point on the path, and to them how they look at life is the only way to do so, but try if you can to view it from a slightly different angle, not necessarily because you want to be seen as the better person, but because hating someone is a heavy load to carry and more harmful to you, than it is to them so you need to put it down. See if you can start each day with a new approach, a happy smiling face and love for yourself and all those around you.

Thank-you Father Benedict.

Family Love

I find myself on the stone bridge that I have walked along before, its lined by my lovely family, it's so good to see them, we smile and hug each other and I would love to stay, and spend time with them but I know that I must not, they line my pathway to give me their love and energies for my work, and as I pass between them and feel their pride, but I do not stay. It's so hard to go, but I do because I see Father Benedict in the distance, sitting on our bench beside the stone wall. I approach him, we sit in comfortable silence and these words are given to me.

Be Open

Be open to receive all the good that comes your way. There will be great leaps forward at times and a standing still at others, you are a physical body and as such there be will demands upon you, the periods of stillness will be times of absorption, to enable you to digest all that's been gathered so far, and to help you to acknowledge your truth. Sometimes you need solitude and other times company, balance in all. With time, rest and play you will then be given opportunities to be off again on your journey but be aware because there is no such thing as coincidence, nothing comes your way by chance, and it's your job to try and work out the lessons within each situation. You may have been busy with the joy of living and not given a lot of thought to things spiritual, or helping others but in truth you will have probably done more than you realise, you let the old lady who only had a few bits of shopping go in front of you in the supermarket queue, you smile and say thank-you and good morning to strangers, you let someone out in traffic, you find a bank statement blowing around in the car park and go out of your way to take it into the bank, because it has so many important personal details on it, you notice an acquaintance at the school gates looking sad and loaded down with troubles, so you invite her little boy home for tea with yours, to give her some time to gather her thoughts, all these things for people you don't really know.

Unknown to you, these kind acts will be stored in your karmic bank account, and as we know there is a return and balance in all things, give out good vibrations with no thought of a return and this will be even more reason for a karmic reward. So be open and aware of everything that's going on around you, because while you are helping others, you are also helping yourself to move forward on your path. When it feels like the old and familiar are changing at a fast speed, be open to the reasons why, you have earned it. Sometimes things just no longer fit the person you have become, so it's time for a leap forward, go with it, it may feel uneasy and scary but in truth things will come to you at the very time, your ears are ready to hear instead of just listening, and your eyes are truly able to see.

Thank-you Father Benedict.

Autumn

It's autumn and we meet outside, I notice as we pass by that although the trees are quite bare there are still a few with lovely red apples on them. We walk over to where the Fathers have their little bedrooms, Father Benedict knocks on the first heavy door we come to and he goes in, I follow and wait just inside the door, there we find one of the Father's sick in bed. Father Benedict picks up an earthenware jug and pours some liquid into a mug, but before he gives it to him, he closes his eyes and silently says a prayer over the mug, he then goes to the Father helps him to sit up and drink the liquid which I know is made from honey and herbs, he then helps him to lie down again, gives more silent prayers and we leave.

Bless Your Food and Drink

In this hurried world you find yourself in, I wonder how many people sit down at the table to eat their first meal of the day, breakfast, it has this name because this is what you are doing, breaking your fast. You will have fasted overnight while you were sleeping and now it's time to begin your day with nourishment and water. How many eat while on the go, a piece of toast in one hand while dashing around and doing with the other, and how many miss it altogether, no time! False economy. Get up half an hour earlier sit down at your table, if you have a family with them, and if not still sit down, say a little prayer over your food if this is your practice, or just silently hold your bowl in your hands and give thanks for it, and be grateful that you can because a lot can't. By doing this you will be helping to raise the vibrations of the food with your healing hands and good intent, to eat or drink anything that has been blessed and therefore had its vibrations raised and the molecules changed will provide you with so much more in the way of nutritional value. In the past food and drink were never eaten unless it had first been blessed and given thanks for, it certainly doesn't have to be a lengthy process. If you are cooking for yourself or for your family bless it at each stage, so that by the time it reaches your mouth it will be alive with so many good vibrations. Try to remember to bless your food every day especially in times of illness or after an operation, so many are happy to leave things completely in the hands of the healthcare givers, when there is such a lot people can do to help themselves as well. Once you begin eating again make sure it's good healthy foods that will feed your cells and organs to make you fit and well, it's no good relying on sugary drinks or snacks for, they will do you no good and, in some cases, will harm your progress or halt it altogether. An example, a young man was recovering from a serious operation, at first, he was going along slowly but nicely and making steady progress, and his appetite improved but because he'd had a lifetime of bad eating habits this is what he now craved, so he indulged himself. He was so relieved to be on the mend and feeling much better that he gave in to his cravings, rationalising I've been through such a lot so I'll treat myself, and he did with chocolate, cake and crisps without a piece of fruit or vegetables in sight. Not all that long after these episodes he started to slip backwards, caught lots of colds which knocked him off his feet again, was constantly tired, cold, miserable and now depressed as well because he wasn't doing as well as he had been, he felt poorly most of the time, slept a lot and when he woke thought I just feel so bad I need a little treat, so coffee and a whole packet of biscuits because he was hungry, and didn't have the energy to prepare any proper foods. Stop! You have been given a second chance, why do you not rejoice, why are you slowly killing yourself, you have a loving family and you owe it to them and yourself to get well. You would not put sub-standard petrol into your car and expect it to perform correctly, so how on earth will your body recover and function at its best when treating it in this way. It's no great mystery, take a deep breath and start again, drink water because you need to re-hydrate, drink it cold to refresh you or warm with honey to soothe you, eat fresh fruit and vegetables in all shapes and sizes and learn how to cook again, don't just grab anything because you are hungry, prepare before and get organised, it doesn't take a lot of time. People have busy lives now, well they've always had busy lives, go to bed half an hour earlier and get up half an hour earlier to prepare your food for the day, your body will thank you for this, it will reward you by being pain free, alert, healthy and full of energy once again. Our talk has finished so we hug, get up and then go our separate ways.

Thank-you Father Benedict.

Look After Yourself

The need to be is more important than the need to do. To do is to escape, to be is to face your fears. The need to do is to surround oneself with distractions and the need to be is to face the reality of one-self. If you do not deal with the necessary – the self, how will you ever find the time to deal with the unnecessary- all the other things in life. To be of service and to help others find a more peaceful way of leading their lives is a wonderful thing to do, but not at the expense of one's own physical or emotional health. Everybody has the same amount of energy and it's their free will how they choose to use it, you could be the kind of person who is like the mouse, whiskers and nose a twitching, dashing around here there and everywhere, or you could be as the elephant, slow methodical and plodding, but just as good at getting the job done. Some are lucky and understand energy because they listen to their bodies and make their decisions with care, take the hare and the tortoise for example, why waste so much precious energy when the outcome is the same, everyone will at some point reach the finish line.

You are a beautiful person and have nothing to prove to yourself or anyone else, so care for yourself as much as you care for others, be loving and kind and do not deplete your energies or leave yourself open to fatigue or illness, rest, because if you don't do it willingly nature has a way of doing it for you.

Life is not a competition and you have nothing to prove, so of course help when you have energy to do so but if you are feeling tired you have the right to say no. life is a balance and it's more about enjoying the journey and not the destination. Take care of your precious body because no one else knows how to do a better job of it than you.

Thank-you Father Benedict.

Spring

I fly very slowly over to the island, our island. It is spring and everything is beginning to come to life again after its winter's sleep which has been a much-needed time for reflection, contemplation and rest. There are new lambs jumping around in the lush green fields, there is expectancy in the air and a feeling of good things to come. I see Father Benedict walking towards me carrying a new born lamb; he's taking the lamb while one of the other Fathers leads the Mother into the barn, so they can be warm and cosy and out of the crisp air.

The Circle of Life
As one new life enters the world elsewhere another is departing, it's the circle of life and it continues ever onwards. It's important to know that no one ever departs the world on their own, there will always be a loving family member there with them to hold their hand. Sometimes the earth family may not be present and for them this cause's pain and regret, because they mistakenly think they were all alone when they "died", but rest assured this is not the case. For a little while the person who is about to pass over will have their feet in both worlds, and as their time draws near they will still be able to hear their earth family's words of comfort and love, but may not always respond, they will also be catching a glimpse of their spirit family and be overjoyed at meeting them again after so long. The love from their family will be on such a strong vibration that they will have little power to resist and will want to join them, especially if the time leading up to this moment has been troublesome. They will unknown to a lot of the earth family members have a say in when the exact time of their departing will be, and often choose a moment when you are unable to be around the bedside or have stepped out for a brief while, it is then they decide to let go completely to spare the agony of the final separation. Of course, there is no real separation it's only that they have gone on ahead, but for the earth family they will feel a great sense of loss as the vibration of the soul passes over and it leaves the body or overcoat, which will then be

lying empty upon the bed and will be felt by the earth family as a huge sense of emptiness and loss. In a lot of cases they will want to spare their loved ones the pain of severing the bonds of earth love and cutting the silver cord that unites the soul with the body. However, it will be felt as a great sense of love a very short time after as the spirit family fills the empty space with the love and healing for them. After a period of adjustment, the newly passed person will be able to be around them again even if only for short bursts of time, and you will be able to recognise them by their vibrational energy which won't have changed.

If this has happened to you it's entirely normal to feel upset or regret for being absent, but please don't because it was your loved one's choice to exit in this way. Sometimes they choose to stay and be with their loving family until their last breath, mainly because of lack of understanding on their part, they will be afraid of the separation thinking this is the end, and there will be no more loving contact, so they are reluctant to leave believing I don't want to let them go, I just can't leave them, they don't realise that once the settling in period has taken place, the two on either side of the glass can still maintain and share the deep love they always did, and in a lot of cases that love and understanding only deepens with time and space. It's important to understand these facts as it makes the transition more bearable for all concerned.

Thank-you Father Benedict.

Energy Thieves

Sometimes without realising what they are doing people will be taking energy from others, they won't realise this, and neither will their victim, as it is all done unconsciously on another plane of thought. The victim will usually be a kind and compassionate sort of person, who likes to help and has a caring nature, the energy thief won't be a bad person at all, just someone who hasn't been taught to give a lot of consideration to the feelings of others, and a lot of this way of thinking will stem from earth family patterns. They will have watched their parents struggle with finances, love, and life in general and be happy to rely on others for help, all the while not changing their thought process, words or actions, and will be stuck in the "poor me" syndrome, "what have I done to deserve this" and "nothing ever works out for me". Well actually anyone could ask those questions, but in order to help yourself to move on, you have to broaden your outlook somewhat. The energy thief will give the impression of someone who is self-reliant and quietly confident, and will be to a certain degree, but in order to fulfil their destiny they will need a certain vulnerability about them to attract the right sort of person, who will just love to take care of people, this too will be part of their family pattern. The energy victim will be happy to give, although they would on occasions like something back, but unfortunately not a lot will be returned to them because it's just not there to give, so after a period of time the well of love begins to dry up, it has no choice because with no rain running into it, and someone constantly dipping their cup in to drink from it, pretty soon there is nothing left, but the two of them will still continue with their patterns of behaviour, but because the energy thief won't be aware of the problem the victim must, it being now time to recognise and conserve one's own energy, time to plug that leak and stop any more from draining away. Once the victim has this realisation, they will never go back to their old way of thinking or being, because no one can "save" anyone else, awareness is uniquely personal.

Thank-you Father Benedict.

In the Barn

Today I find myself inside the barn, I see the Fathers milking the goats. To one side is a barrel on some sort of wooden structure, I watch as Father Thomas is turning the handle to make butter. (I haven't had the name of another Father before, this is nice) as I sit on the bale of hay, I wonder what we'll talk about today.

Answers from Within
There has never been a better time for knowledge, and there are so many ways for people to learn just about anything they desire, however, for some technology can be quite overwhelming so the simple ways of learning are still needed, getting quiet and seeking answers from within, meditating and reaching out to the universe are ways that have been used for a very long time, and still work well today. Link in with the ancestors, for there is nothing new and nothing they haven't seen before, or had to deal with themselves at some point, also answers to all questions are to be found in the great halls of learning, where there are volumes of books to access, the name for them are the Akashic records. Every soul has a record which is updated by you each time you return home, over many lifetimes you begin to build up vast quantities of knowledge, all of life's adventures, tasks and problems are here for future reference. Advancement of the soul takes a lot of lifetimes and there is no rush, slow and steady is always best, otherwise you will miss things and will need to attend to them again later. There are many things you will need answers to, one for example may be, I'd like to help people but I'm unsure of the best way to go about it, begin by getting into the quiet and ask your question, you will always be guided to the right time, place, situation or circumstance and you must trust your gut feelings, this is probably one of the hardest things to do, especially if you had some idea of how you were going to go about things, but be open to change and all possibilities. You may be guided to take a study course, and you may start to use the information you have learned so far, and then for some reason it all comes to a halt, you might then be guided to go in another direction, or so it seems to

you, you start this project and carry on fine for a while, only to find this ends too. You must realise that no knowledge is ever wasted and it is all part of a bigger plan, perhaps you are trying out all these things to see which one suits you best. You may even stop all your learning for a while to give your soul, spirit or higher consciousness time to absorb and piece together, what's been gathered so far, and once your understanding has reached a certain level, you'll find that you are again guided to go back to the original studies, but now with a different perspective on how to apply them all. The original information was correct, but now with your higher perspective the results you gain will be more advanced, but however you choose to gain your knowledge for helping yourself and others, you will find that the more you know, the more you realise that, you don't really know very much at all, but still keep "searching for your own answers" for they are always there.

Thank- you Father Benedict.

On the Island

Today when I arrive on the island, the north wind is blowing and there's snow on the ground, but despite how cold I am I can still appreciate the beauty of it all, it's a magical winter wonderland, all sparkly and new. I then make my way quickly to the barn where I find it cosy and warm inside, the animals are here, and Father Andrew is milking a goat.

Retrain your Mind

Whenever a negative thought comes into your head, be aware and try to halt it in its tracks. Everything that exists does so because of firstly the thought, then the word and finally the action, so learn to be selective. Train your mind as you would your dog, to walk nicely on the lead, pull it back with gentle assertiveness, your dog is eager to be on it's way so it tries to run ahead with only one thought, to get there as quickly as possible, so it doesn't notice the old lady walking quietly along loss in her thoughts and knocks her over, he doesn't see or hear the cars going by and is surprised when one beeps it's horn in warning, as he steps onto the road. Do not let your dog or your thoughts race along so madly that the collar pulls tight around the neck, choking the life out of you and leaving you both feeling exhausted, and when you do finally stop and turn around, you see you haven't travelled very far at all despite your best efforts. You teach your dog to walk to heel so teach your mind to do the same; you take your puppy to classes to help to make it aware of the dangers of being out in public places, so take your mind to classes too. Put your mind on a harness or restraint , it will greatly benefit you and those around you when life gets hectic, try to sit quietly and just be, call it relaxation ,meditation, mindfulness or being in the now, try five or ten minutes at first and be as patient with yourself as you would be your pup. The mind and the pup will run away at first especially if there is a nice distraction but be gentle on both because nothing worth having was ever gained at speed, slow and steady is the key to a happy and contented life. Competition has its place and that's on the track and field not in life itself, there will always be someone who is quicker, smarter, prettier or taller than you and that's just how it is, so don't compare yourself to anyone its pointless, be pleased that you are unique and be proud of your own achievements and abilities, unknown to you, others are looking your way and wishing they had your good looks, brain or personality and you would probably be very surprised to hear this and say "who me?" Never forget everyone is great in their own way.

Thank-you Father Benedict.

You all Help Each Other, Whether you Realise it or Not

Every day as you interact with each other you are learning, sharing knowledge and helping each other to grow whether intentional or not. An example, a lady who was in the caring profession had very sadly loss her husband and hadn't been able to work for a while, but she still had her bills to pay, so even though she wasn't ready to return to work, she did so.

She was caring for an elderly lady who couldn't do a lot for herself any more, which made her upset and feel quite useless, she felt she hadn't anything to contribute to anyone and often felt depressed. The carer felt she must be professional and hid her emotions especially the tears when they came, but on one occasion the lady found her hiding in the bathroom, unable to stop them, she pulled her into her arms and let her cry until she was done. Once she had regained her composure, she felt very guilty, here was this dear lady who was so dependant upon others reversing the roles, she tried to say she was sorry, but the old lady just smiled and said thank you, the younger lady was puzzled. You have made me feel useful again, there is not much I can do for others any more so to be able to hug and comfort you, has made me feel like a real person again. The carer was taken aback, then she also smiled and said thank you, I need to stay strong in front of my children and other family members, because I know they are so worried about me, but today I could just be me, and let it all out, thank you so much. They hugged once more, and it felt good to know they were each helping the other. Love is always around you, whether you realise this or not.

Thank-you Father Benedict.

Morning Prayers

Today when we meet the bell is ringing for early morning prayers. I watch the Fathers and the Brothers walk into the chapel with their heads bowed in silence. Father Benedict bids me follow, and I sit quietly on my own at the back. I feel very privileged.

Spread the Love
All things about earth life must be experienced by each person for full understanding and completion, but they will not run in any order. You may be experiencing a life of relative ease and comfort, in both material aspects and physical, you may be living a life of wealth where everything ticks along very nicely, you have good health, great friends and family and a disposable income, but please remember that everyone is not that lucky, so you will still need to keep your heart open to others, for your own advancement, as well as helping them.

There are so many dimensions in time, and each one is being lived simultaneously, and needs to be experienced, so if you haven't for example had a life of hardship yet, perhaps a setting in Victorian London along with its poverty and disease will be your next challenge. All events are there to help you to grow in compassion and kindness, and to help you understand what it means to walk in someone else's shoes. Help each other out in any small way that you can, pass on what you no longer need, clothes or books because they may be just what somebody else is looking for, leave a few cans of pet food in the donation box at the supermarket, or give a pound or two to a local charity. Don't necessarily buy the man on the street a cup of coffee, he might not like coffee, and besides he may need that bottle to keep out the nights cold, or to escape his sad life for a while, and return to spirit where he has no worries, please do not judge him because you do not know him, or what brought him to the place where he finds himself now. Do whatever you can, for the sake of all concerned including yourself, help to build your own karmic bank account because next time around, if it's you sitting on the banks of the river Thames, cold, hungry and miserable, and a kind stranger gives you a few pennies, you'll be so glad that you did.

Backwards in time, forward in health, forwards in time or backward in compassion, it doesn't necessarily run in any order, but providing you leave each life with more love than when you entered, that is progression for your soul. Each occurrence in every lifetime must be dealt with correctly, don't just shut your eyes and hope it will turn out alright, because unless you inject some love into everything it can't. Love is the antidote to all of life's problems, and love is the only way to view all souls and situations, not everyone will have the same breaks or opportunities pass their way, some do have hardships so be compassionate and do what you can to help them. One small act of kindness can change someone's life. Love reaches far beyond your own front door.

Thank You, Father Benedict...

Make Love

How a person is created has a large impact on how they will view the world and interact with other people. If the parent's relationship was stormy and there were many arguments, these factors will be transferred to the sperm and the egg, even before the fertilisation process begins. The emotions are carried through the body in all the cells, so couples who have relations to try to make things better between them, or even worse the man takes the woman against her will, either inside or outside of the relationship, will not lead to a fully functioning baby being created. The anger, the hurt and the resentment will all be transferred to the DNA of the embryo, and the child will develop and grow at a different rate, both inside of the womb and out. Unfortunately, their view of the world will also be a little tarnished, they won't always be able to see the good in people, and will think they have an ulterior motive, for the nice things they do. They won't always be able to feel love, they will to their own minds feel it, and give it, but it will be on a different level to how others interpret love. It is true that everyone views the world from their own perspective, and from the events that have helped to shape who they are, but these poor souls will be at a disadvantage even before they emerge into the living world. They will usually be quite insular and self-absorbed, making most situations they encounter about themselves, empathy and sympathy will also be at a lower level if at all. They will find that a lot of the time they are angry with the world and not quite in step with everyone else, and this will be true because the anger, resentment and negative feelings that were present in their creation will have been transferred to them. Of course, these brave souls will have consented to the parents and conditions of conception, before they came into the physical form, for they like everyone will need to experience all that earth life has to offer.

If however, a baby has been created out of love and respect for each other, the parents wanting to show tenderness and consideration, this love will also be transferred, once again via the egg and the sperm, and this moment of conception will be the starting point for the love, the sympathy and the empathy of how this baby will view the world, and the people in it. It is so important when creating a child, how both parents feel about each other, in the vast majority of cases, children will be created from love and grow up in a loving environment, they are the lucky ones, but if a child is made from two unhappy, uncaring parents then this factor alone, will shape how they view the world from conception onwards, so do not make a child out of resentment, anger or frustration but out of love.

Thank-you Father Benedict.

Swimming in Cold Water

I find myself alone at the shoreline and the tide is in. It's a bright sunny day with a lovely clear blue sky, the gulls are calling to each other and everything feels perfect. I stand and look around, there is no one here. I know I must go across to the other side, nothing else for it but to swim. The water's cold and takes my breath away but it's a short distance so off I go. When I reach the other shore Father Benedict is there waiting with a soft blanket to put around me, we sit on the sand and these are the thoughts I am given.

Affirmations

These are little sayings a lot like prayers that people utter to themselves, usually first thing in the morning before they start their day, to ensure that all goes well. They are little reminders to help to keep themselves positive, by repeating them daily they become ingrained into the subconscious or higher conscious and help them to become who they want to be. They are affirming to themselves to look at all the great things that life has to offer, repetition is one of the easiest ways to keep a person positive, because you become the vibration of the words. You can affirm to your higher-self anything you wish for example, I am healthy, this will be vibrating at a high frequency that transfers the thought in turn to the physical body, so any invaders will be at a loss to penetrate the defence lines, your high frequency thoughts are like little soldiers on guard. You could affirm, "I am love", or "my body is a magnet for love", or "I love everyone and everyone loves me", and those that don't will be vibrating at a frequency so much lower than the one you will be on, that you won't even notice them and they will simply pass you by. By stating these affirmations every morning, you will attract and give out love to the world and every person you are in contact with. Love is all powerful, there is no greater vibration to have or release, and by adding your smile it will increase even more. Others may include, "I am content", or "nothing or no one can change this wonderful vibration I feel right now", and this is true because no one can change your vibration, that's down to you if you do not remain in this happy place, no one has any power over you unless you give it to them, but just one little falter will be enough for some of their energy to penetrate yours. Be poised, be positive and be protected by your loving affirmations. There is a need to rise above all the negativity of the world, so high that nothing or no one can effect what you have worked so hard to achieve, as you begin to understand how the universe works you grow spiritually and you realise that as you help others you also help yourself, your aura will become lighter and brighter and you will be a joy to be around, people will want to share in the love that you send out. Your thoughts become your words and your words become your actions. So, set your day and start with a high frequency affirmation and observe just how much your life will change for the better.

Thank-you Father Benedict.

A Time of Action

I am so excited to be moving forward again after a period of much needed rest. We will all have times of action and times of rest, when the new knowledge is properly processed and understood. Sometimes the resting periods will be because of illness, but there is such a lot you can do to help yourself.

Self-Healing for Mind, Body and Spirit
Begin, – Sit quietly and undisturbed and have to hand anything that you feel you need at this time, it may be different on each occasion just listen to your inner voice, it may be a particular crystal or crystals, flowers or a potted plant, sea shells or pebbles or even a piece of drift wood, each will be sending out its own vibration that will instantly feel right when you hold it. A glass of water and a lighted candle to remind yourself that you always work on a vibration of love. Perhaps the crystals will be placed at your feet or held in your hands or placed in your lap, whatever feels right, is right. Have pleasant music to drift away to and breathe.

To begin with a few cleansing breaths, slow and deep, then your normal pattern of breathing, and when you feel calm and comfortable speak to yourself gently and say "I release all of the tension that I hold inside my body, I slowly and purposefully let it go, I drop my shoulders, unclench my jaw and my lips, my head feels well balanced upon my shoulders and my tummy is calm and holds no knots, my legs and feet are grounded and I am well supported on the chair, I feel warm and comfortable. Then breathe and smile to yourself on the inside as well as the outside, and affirm to yourself, I now forgive myself for the negative thoughts, fears and judgements I may have been holding inside for myself or for others, breathe and feel relaxed and calm, I release all past patterns that no longer serve me and are holding me back from peace and happiness. I now breathe love into my heart to fill the space these patterns have left. There is no room for anything but love and light. I see and understand the reasons for what has happened in the past and know there is no need for me to look at anything, with those eyes again. My mind body and spirit will heal itself as I gently let go, there is nothing for me to do as it will happen naturally once I'm in alignment with love. There is no blame or judgement on myself or anyone else, as we were only working with the knowledge we had at the time, I now look with kind eyes and feel at peace.

Thank-you Father Benedict.

By the Coast

It's a lovely day as I walk towards the island, I see Father Benedict collecting seaweed for the kitchen, and so I pick up a spare basket and fall into step beside him.

Mind over Matter

The spirit is strong but the flesh is weak, that's because the spirit has seen and experienced many things before, where-as this is always the first time for the flesh. So, although your mind may tell you something and you agree, when it comes to putting it into practice that's another story completely. It's easy to believe that you will listen to that little voice inside that says, that is the last time I'm going to have that much to drink, I feel so bad today it's just never worth it, look how much money I spent last night, or I feel so guilty for eating that much chocolate cake, but it is so hard to resist, or I really should not have spent that much money on new clothes, but I get carried away with my credit cards, I won't do it again I promise, and you really mean it when you say these things, but the flesh is weak and temptation is hard to resist. There is no wrong if it feels right to the individual, and resonates to your truth but, if you keep having regrets and your head is in a constant state of turmoil then this will have a detrimental effect on your wellbeing. The flesh is physical and needs stimulation, but the spirit doesn't, because it doesn't need material things to sustain it, for it knows all gratification's like these are fleeting, and once over leave you wanting more, where-as mindful actions will feed the soul and help with its growth, mindfulness deals with the now and makes ready for the future.

Thank-you Father Benedict.

Leap of Faith

A lot of people will wait their whole lives just hoping that "life" will happen. They realise what they have is okay, but they also know it could be a whole lot better, so what do they do? Nothing, they wait, and they hope.

There is no such thing as coincidence, and everything that comes your way is there for a reason, to see whether your ears, eyes and hearts are open or whether you are stumbling around in the dark. Be awake to all that's presented to you and if something magical comes your way grab it, it's been sent so that you may take a leap of faith. Sometimes these occurrences will be given to see how brave you are, or how much you really want what you think you want, a little test for you, the universe can see what will happen in both sets of circumstances but of course the final decision will always be yours. Sometimes the little tests or leaps of faith will seem scary, but if you can be logical about it and view it as if it's not yours, this may make it a bit easier to decide. Nothing that comes your way is random it's all part of the truth that you believe on some level of your understanding, especially when you feel stuck and negative about what you are experiencing this time. Everything is part of a bigger picture and one that you will not be fully aware of at this moment, that's why it's called a leap of faith, you will have been standing on the very edge of something, waiting for who knows what to happen, but before it can you need to gather all your strength and go for it because to remain standing still means nothing will change, so either resign yourself to this or when the opportunity arises then jump, into who knows what, but you will have at least changed the circumstances you were in and it might just be the best move you will ever make.

Thank-you Father Benedict.

The Causeway

Once again, I find myself at the causeway, this time the tide is slowly going out and starting to reveal the tiny stones and pebbles that line the way, I bend down to have a closer look, they are so pretty, especially the shiny wet amber and gold coloured ones. They glisten in the sun but once they start to dry in my hand, they don't look so attractive, so I lower my hand back into the water once again and look more intently at them, as I stare my eyes begin to glaze over, and I'm lost in my thoughts, my imagination.... In my mind's eye they become anything I want them to be, little pieces of gold, little blobs of golden honey or specks of sunshine.

Imagination

Your imagination is one of the best gifts that you possess and probably one of the least understood. For a lot of people imagination or pretend is something that children do when they are playing, they imagine that they are driving a train, or they are a king or queen or a superhero, so they reason that because it's imagination it's not real, it's make-believe and therefore untrue. Because the mind of a child is pure and not distorted by life they can with all their heart make their game a real event, they can see their train and they can be the king or queen without any difficulty, to them there is no difference, they see it in their minds eye so it's as real as if they were to see it with their physical eye, what a shame this beautiful gift gets lost as you grow. An adult will observe and marvel at the child's ability to imagine and think it's a sweet thing, and even comment "it's just their imagination", as if that makes it somewhat less, whereas if this gift were nurtured instead of believing it was something that you grew out of, adult life could go along a whole lot smoother. For every event that occurs in your life will have started in your mind or your thoughts, so think how much better your current position might be if you had been taught to control those random thoughts and imagined them to be good ones instead of letting them fly about in your head, at a hundred miles an hour. If you actually did think, if you choose your thoughts and let your imagination see yourself achieving great things, if you saw yourself in the happiest of relationships instead of just hoping things would work out, if you imagined in your mind's eye being successful in your chosen career, making lots of money and living a very comfortable lifestyle, if you allowed your thoughts to go in the direction of abundance instead of fingers crossed, and then allowed yourself to feel proud of your achievements, but for some strange reason people are made to feel boastful if they are successful, why? Success comes down to believing in yourself, and successful people haven't lost the ability to see or imagine themselves achieving great things. Nothing is impossible and no task to big, greatness cannot be accomplished by negative thinking, and even if you don't yet fully believe in the power of thought, or in the imagination, pretend that you do, be as a child again and make believe. Pretend you have what you wish for, and that you have it right now, the more you do this the more your thoughts will catch up with the pretence and make it happen, if your words also join in this adds to the positive vibrations that make the action occur. You can make your life any way you choose with your thoughts, imagination, words and actions. See it, believe it and live it.

Thank-you Father Benedict.

Attitudes

Your attitude to life plays an enormous role in creating or destroying the health of your body. Your attitudes and feelings towards the people you share your lives will affect you in a big way. It doesn't or shouldn't matter what they give out and it is up to you how you respond or deal with it. If you want to remain healthy you must remain unaffected and realise its only their perception of life as it is with anyone, they will be operating from their past and their childhood backgrounds. Just because others see the world in a certain way it doesn't mean you have to, or respond with hurt or anger because their words or actions are different to yours, and have caused you to feel upset, you owe it to yourselves not to let their view change yours especially if it's a negative one, on the other hand if their view is a positive one it may just be showing you a better way of looking at life, so try to keep open minded to whatever comes your way. Your job, and it's quite a hard one when you first hear this, is to try to remain neutral, your inside world makes your outside world, meaning, how you feel will affect your health and wellbeing. If you constantly feel unappreciated, unseen or even unloved this will have a huge impact on the state of your health, if you don't have a lot of confidence or self-esteem because for example you grew up with a parent, or family member who didn't praise you or had a very loving or demonstrative nature, you may have felt misunderstood or rejected in some way, unknowingly you let their negative vibrations into your aura or personal space. You cannot afford to let anyone's opinion of you, have any bearing on how you feel about yourself, which is not an easy task when you're a child, or indeed how you feel about them because harbouring any hurt, feelings of not being good enough or humiliation will lead to an unhappy spirit and in turn an unhappy body, developing into a dis-ease later on. Having a contented life is essential for a healthy life, all that you are is a direct result of your thoughts, so realise other people's judgements are just that, their judgements and not yours, so don't give away your power, don't give away your happiness or your health. Your attitude is your key to all the good that can come your way, so make it a good one.

Thank-you Father Benedict.

The Breathing Sea

I find myself sitting on a low wall near to the sea with Father Benedict, we're listening to the waves lapping very gently in and out like the breath of all that is, it's soothing to the ear, I think of the sound of the Mother's breathing when the child is inside the womb, comforting, warm and safe, we sit in silence, and then I say "I have a question please."

Why do Friendships Wax and Wane?
It seems that for the longest period of time you can be partners or best friends with someone and you completely "get" each other. You finish each other's sentences, say the same things at the same time and laugh about it, you just feel so at ease in their company, and then for some strange reason it all changes. You find each other irritating, what you say seems to grate on their nerves and they find they disagree with almost all you are saying. In fact time spent together is fraught and no longer fun, and even at times uncomfortable. Why is this?

Answer: Simply put, the vibrations between you are out of sync and you are not on the same page any more, you irritate them, and you get upset by their remarks, your vibrations are just not a match any more because you have moved in different directions, perhaps one of you is still seeing the world as you did together, and one has had their eyes opened just a little more and neither of you will understand why. In situations as this the best thing to do is give each other some space for there is no point in being upset and spoiling a perfectly good long- term friendship or relationship. No one is ever standing still, energy is constantly moving and changing and what was a match today is a mismatch tomorrow, it happens in all relationships whether platonic romantic or family, they are always changing. Everything has a cycle to it, a time to come alive and a time to die down, the moon will wax and wane, sometimes it will shine so bright in the night sky, and sometimes you will hardly see it because of the clouds, but it will still be there just like you will be, if or when your friend or family member needs you and vice-versa. The fire in your grate will burn bright and warm, and then die down unless you give it more energy in the form of coal or wood, the fuel it needs to get ignited again, it's just the same with all your relationships, people come in and out of your life when you're on the same vibrational wave length, and you give to each other the fuel to keep it alive, and when you're not it's ok to let the friendship die down for a while and wait until the time is right for it to glow brightly again.

Thank-you Father Benedict.

Spring Again

It's Spring and I find I'm in a small meadow with lovely spring flowers nodding their heads in the warm breeze, I recognise some of them, yellow daisies and dandelion, white ox-eyed daisies, blue cornflowers and forget me knots. I see Father Benedict gathering some nettles to make tea.

Self Sufficient

It's your job as parents to teach your children to be self-sufficient, show them all the skills you have so they will be able to live a fully independent life. If you do too much for them you will hinder their growth, you must be there to love and to guide, to protect and nurture, to cherish and to teach but also to stand back and let them find their own way. You cannot try to correct the "mistakes" from your own childhood through them either, for the simple reason they key players are all different now, your parents are out of the equation and your children are in, so it wouldn't work, all the energies will be different, and the lessons were for you and not for them. This is one reason why parents cannot expect their children to follow in the family footsteps or go into the family business, unless they want to because the jobs were your choices and not necessarily theirs, so they wouldn't be putting all their love and dedication into it. You cannot try to recapture your lost opportunities through them, longing for the chance to change the past will only bring heartache, nothing is wrong or wasted, it just is. You must always love them for who they are instead of who you want them to be, and you will make them feel inferior if you're forever "showing" them the right way, for there is no right or wrong way just an individual point of view.

No one should be dependent on anyone, for at such times as you are gone from their lives your children will be completely lost, it will be painful enough for them with the physical separation of a hand to hold or a body to hug but if they also have to contend with not knowing how to live an independent life as well their heartbreak will be unbearable. Guide and teach but do not overwhelm or take away their lessons, for when you have

42

gone spirit-side you too will be upset to see what you have helped to create. Everyone must live their lives according to their own rules, obviously that doesn't mean living that life in a thoughtless, mean or self- indulgent way, it means you are the only one who knows what's best for you, and by having a solid grounding from your parents you have enough confidence to try. Everyone makes many "mistakes" along the way and some will be painful, but with each pain comes new understanding and unless you experience it for yourself it will never resonate in your soul. You can be told how pleasurable it is to eat a piece of chocolate and have it explained in detail, but it will not make sense to you until you feel it melt in your mouth.

A good parent is one that's not needed, loved of course, respected and cared for yes, but not needed, when you give your child their wings, they will happily fly back to you, but if you keep them clipped once they do leave the nest, they will be lost to you. Being a parent is the hardest and most rewarding job there is.

Thank-you Father Benedict.

Don't Look for Love

To be held in someone's arms is wonderful, to make love can be heavenly but to risk all for this is a little bit short sighted. There are so many parts to a happy relationship, so don't go headlong into an encounter just because the physical side is great, get to know the person and their personality first, because while making love is nice it's not the whole package and if that's all you see then that's all you'll get. If you are in a rush for a relationship you will be attracting people who are also in a rush, they will come in, spin you around, make you dizzy with all sorts of promises, which at the time they will mean but won't keep, and while you are slowing things down again to your own natural rhythm they will be rushing out again, fed up with your slow pace. You will not have lived up to their view of the world, they aren't looking for slow and comfortable like you are they are looking for excitement, thrills with no commitment to home life and all the boring routines that go with it, they will still want to be out adventure seeking, and if you don't go along with their view they will do it anyway. If you want commitment, dependability and a lasting relationship then slow and steady is the only way, you may have reached a point in your life where you think that time is slipping away from you, so you'll have to be quick before it's too late, but don't do it because you owe it to yourself and your happiness to get it right. Don't search for anyone or anything, let everything find you in its own good time. How often have you gone to the cupboard looking for what you felt sure was there, you search, turn things out and sort through because you know it's there somewhere, you're certain of it, but you just can't seem to put your finger on it, so you come away frustrated and angry. After a while the anger subsides and you think to yourself ok I'll just get on with what I was doing, and the very next time you go to the cupboard and open it, there it is right under your nose, life is just the same, never search, never plead, never be desperate and what you seek will find you but only when you are in the right frame of mind.

Thank-you Father Benedict.

44

In the Kitchen

Today I find myself in the kitchen watching Father Michael (oh how lovely I have another name) baking bread, but it looks so different to what I know as bread, it's quite flat and it doesn't seem to have risen at all, but it does smell lovely, so homely and comforting. Safe and warm is how it makes me feel, and it reminds me of being in the kitchen with my Mum and Nan all of us cooking together, especially at Christmas time when we all had a stir and a wish of the Christmas puddings. Contented, safe and warm.

Change

I realise that not everyone has been lucky enough to grow up in a safe and loving home with parents and grandparents to love, guide and protect them, so many have a daily fight on their hands just to get by or even to stay alive, their lives are filled with fear and abuse, with difficult days and nights to live through and this is so sad. But no matter what hardship has befallen you there is always a chance to change the outcome if that person has the courage to try. Never forget the care givers in your life are only working with the knowledge available to them at the time, so if their advice or actions are a bit off course there is no blame attached, and hopefully everyone will leave their lives with more wisdom than when they entered it. Change is possible, and patterns do not have to be repeated once they are recognised, so no matter what your circumstances or experiences up to this point, there is another way if you look hard enough. One of the first things to do to enable yourself to move forward is to forgive and not to hold a grudge, however that does not mean condoning or carrying on receiving bad treatment, it means acknowledging that the people who did the dis-service didn't necessarily know what they were doing, so when the bad behaviour begins don't stay and retaliate, if you can, quietly remove yourself. It was written a long time ago "forgive them for they know not what they do", and in most cases it's true, people do not realise the consequences of their words or actions, for when someone is upset or angry words come spilling out with no thought what so ever, sometimes but not always when someone has calmed down they may think how they have hurt or upset others, and depending on their personality will or will not apologise, if they do, this goes some way to appeasing their actions but when they realise their mistakes and still do nothing to rectify things, this will store up even more bad karma for them. In some case's people can be quite abusive in their behaviour towards others with actions as well as words, and not even have one thought of how wrong they are because of family patterns, for them this behaviour is perfectly acceptable and normal but somewhere along the line these family traits should and must change. Everyone is capable of change if they want to engage in a little bit of hard work, to push themselves a little out of the familiar and to accept some challenges because after all said and done, change can be exciting as well. The only way to grow is through love, it's what everyone is searching for, from the school yard bully to the corporate boss. They all want to feel loved.

Thank-you Father Benedict.

Fish Stew

Today I find myself on the shore watching the Fathers collecting cockles, winkles and small clams after the recent rough seas have washed them ashore. They are to be taken to the kitchen along with the seaweed collected, to be made into a fish stew.

Cockles of the Heart
The heart of the seashell is the best part of it, the tough exterior is only the cover for what lies within, and this is no different with people, the body is the overcoat that protects the best part inside, the heart, without it you cannot exist, it is there beating and working hard to keep you alive but also to show you and the world your true essence. The heart is where your spirit and ego meet, and it's there to process every encounter and every decision you make, it is your filter, if your personality is too strongly connected to your mind or ego there won't be a lot of compassion in your actions, your mind will respond logically to encounters and it's this that will keep you in the material, but material possessions can never make up for emotional love and caring. Your car or a wad of cash will never love you back no matter how much care and attention you give to it, but if you can learn to operate from the heart more with compassion, understanding and love for the things that do matter, your family, friends and pets and even yourself, this alone will make you a better person who will get more contentment out of life. The solid materialistic things you lavish your attention on is where the exchange of energies stop, for there is no heart in the material items to make it a full circle and thus return it to you, whereas if you give time and understanding to another not only do they feel worthwhile and loved, but at their centre is beating a heart too that will respond with love and heartfelt gratitude for your kindness and will then be returned to you. The heart is the filter for all that happens in your life so if you listen to it instead of dismissing it you won't go far wrong. The reason people come to earth school is to be able to graduate and leave with more understanding of how life works and

47

know that love is at the heart of everything, so the more you can generate it and feel it the more you will be able to release it for all to enjoy.

Thank-you Father Benedict.

Clairvoyance

We understand that time is an illusion and all the events that have happened and are still to come are all taking place right now, for those people who consciously choose to raise their vibrations to a level of knowing these things are very clear. If you don't yet have the ability yourself and decide to visit a medium or clairvoyant for advice on life, the advice they give won't be "fortune telling" it will be their own clear vision or clairvoyance into the events that could potentially occur if you stay on the path you're travelling on now. It will be more a case of guidance rather than prediction as nothing is set in stone, so if you like what you hear then carry on with the way you are living your life right now, but if you are shown something you don't like the look of this is your opportunity to change your future by changing what's happening in the present moment, you create your future reality by the thoughts, words and actions you have now. The clairvoyance is a wake-up call it's not magic and it's not really a mystery as to how they do it, they will have either brought the gift of clairvoyance with them from a previous lifetime, or their family will have lived with a raised consciousness and they will have observed how their parents and grandparents think, speak and act with compassion and understanding for all. It will be a harder journey if these things are missing because you won't achieve such a high level of love if your thoughts words and actions are low or negative. When you are told that anyone can do it, it's true up to a point, the gift of clairvoyant abilities can be seen to travel down through the generations, but the gift doesn't get passed through the genes like for example hair or eye colour, it gets passed by attitudes and how the children view their parents behaviour, do they give time and love to them and others or are they always too busy, do they teach love and caring through the way they treat the family pets and even how they teach them to play with their teddies and dolls, it's important to start all these things from a young age so it becomes their normal. Are they forever complaining about the world events they see on the news, or do they teach their little ones to be open minded, do they observe you loving your family and friends or do they see quarrels and pettiness, all this will shape your child's future, so if you desire a raised consciousness and therefore way of life, you can do it with love.

How do you or the medium know what your probable future might be? All events forward and backward in time are being played out now, it's a case of sending the consciousness forward to view the events that are taking place and they can do this as their thought pattern and energies are high and are able to project or travel forward in time. People do this when they are sleeping, and also when they are in the process of transitioning when they have a foot in both worlds, an example, a much loved Husband and Father was in this process and would be asleep for long periods of time, upon one of his waking moments he told his family that his favourite football team, the one he had supported all his life were going to win the match they were due to play later on that day, he even gave the score and a few incidences of the game. Not long after this he fell asleep and made his journey, his loving family were obviously very upset and wanted to remain in each other's company for comfort. They went for a walk along the beach together and when they got back to their car's they remembered what he had said, and switched on the radio, lo and behold the score was as he had predicted, as were some of the details of the game, they could not believe what they were hearing. He hadn't wanted to miss his team winning so he projected his spirit forward in time to watch them before he passed permanently, as he knew that once he had done so he would miss it, as his spirit family would be there to welcome him home, settle him in and attend to the healing process that everyone needs on returning home.

Thank-you Father Benedict.

The Monastery Garden

For one of the few times as yet, I find myself sitting in the moonlight with Father Benedict; we are in the monastery grounds sitting on our bench gazing up at the sky. It's a beautiful night not cold at all and very clear, the sky is deep blue and filled with stars, the moon is full and bright. We sit together in comfortable silence, because our Island is small you can hear the sea from almost everywhere, all be it quietly from this point, as it laps gently in and out. It's wonderfully peaceful and calm.

Love is at the Heart of All
This sky is the same sky that man has forever gazed up at in wonder, so many questions and thoughts, are we alone in the universe, is there life on other planets, are there other galaxies, if so do they live as we do, who made the stars and the moon, what magnificent power created all of this and where do I fit in, what's my role or purpose, and am I doing all that I'm supposed to.

Such an array of questions, so loud on the inside and yet so quiet and peaceful on the outside. All these questions will be answered given time and that's something there is plenty of, but as with anything worth investigation slow and steady otherwise the best will be missed. We will cover all these things and many more in our time together for no-body will ever stop learning. The mind is vast, but the heart is bigger, so if everything is viewed with the heart understanding becomes clearer, love is at the heart of all and without it nothing could exist, it's energy in its purest form and when in motion it transfers into matter. Those stars up in the sky that burn so bright, came into being out of the creation of love, at the centre of each atom and molecule is loving energy and we are all made of the same, each structure when delved into will have the same components and it's this loving energy that binds us all together, so when you hear the words you are all brothers and sisters that applies to every animal, plant, rock and tree, nothing is different or separate and it's a big mistake to think otherwise. Every living thing is part of everything else, I am you, you are me and what you do to me you do to yourself, likewise what I do to you I do to myself, there is no ending or beginning there is only now, no past or future only this moment in time, no tomorrow because it never comes, time is an illusion. Each incarnation is continuing from the last so therefore separate in any form simply cannot exist. If everybody could understand this there would be no arguments because how can you argue with yourself, no war, why inflict pain on yourself, no cheating in any form because you would only be cheating yourself, so to give to another you give to yourself, to be kind and loving means you are being kind and loving to yourself as you should be. The sooner everyone wakes up to the fact that separate only exist in the mind of the unenlightened the better it will be for the whole of mankind.

Thank-you Father Benedict.

Protect and Transmute

Father Benedict tells me everybody needs to learn how to protect themselves from the negative energies that can slow your progression, spiritual growth and ease your daily life. Unfortunately there is a lot out there, and it will affect you if you allow it, or if you don't know how to stop it.

To let negativity rest within you or upon you can reveal itself as a physical problem, particularly back and shoulder ache because you are literally shouldering the burdens of negativity, so get into the habit of putting yourself in a bubble of protection each morning to stop yourself from absorbing everything that comes your way. As you get better at taking care of yourself and become more spiritually aware, realise the bubble will transmute as well as protect, it will turn negative energies into positive ones, learn to call upon your higher self or higher consciousness to help you to sum up people and situations. If your light shines bright you will in fact draw things to you because you will have the ability to cope with, and to sort out other people and situations. Your higher self will be able to connect to the higher self of the other person, to help to show them a better more peaceful way of dealing with manmade problems, you yourself will not always be aware of what to do or say, but your higher consciousness will have witnessed many situations like these before and will know the correct way of dealing with them. You will be called upon to be a shining light of inspiration to help the world move to a higher level in order for it to survive, and you can only do this if you have the knowledge of protection, the first rule in helping anyone is as always, take care of yourself because if you don't adhere to this you will have little chance of helping others. Meditate to see things clearly and to keep them in proportion, to have a better understanding of earth life as it is, find peace within and then without and learn to be less effected by all people and situations, realise that you can deal with the things you can change, but if you can't change them bless them for their lessons and leave them to pass by, the more love and understanding you can give the more peaceful you'll become along with the people you affect, because the more love they receive the less dense the energy they will carry. Be a beacon of love and light because the world needs more light workers like all of you, who have been guided to read these words.

Thank-you Father Benedict.

In the Monastery

Today I find myself inside the monastery watching Father Benedict at his book work; here I see lovely cream parchment paper and beautiful handwriting which is very detailed and artistic.

Ancient Philosophies

There have always been people who have chosen to give themselves to the service of love; it is the key to life itself for without it there is no life. The communication of knowledge is wisdom in the making. A single grain of sand when joined with other grains becomes the mountain, and a single drop of water when joined with other drops becomes the ocean, no one person can achieve great change on their own but when joined with all other like-minded people can transform the world into a better place for all to live in. There have always been throughout your history people who seek to change by conquering and possessing, in their own eyes changing the world, but unfortunately to bring about change by force is pointless because unless things are given freely, they will always return to where they came from. Love is only love when it's given freely and to try to obtain by any other means just won't work, you may try with flattery, gifts or compliments or even force, but unless things are given from a place of love they will wither and die, change can only happen from a place of love. When one comes across information of change it's never by accident, it comes to you on the same level of understanding that you already possess, so if it does come from a higher or lower level it will simply pass you by. Once the information has been absorbed and fully understood, it's the duty of the individual to pass it on in the form of communication to others and it is a commitment not to be taken lightly, it is a responsibility so unless you intend to see it through you must not start it. When we observe you actively taking part in service and making a difference to others lives we will continue to bring people and situations to you, so you may help more people and in doing so help yourself also. If at any time you feel over-whelmed, you only need say, and we will slow things down until you have caught up and feel full of energy again. Service comes in many forms listening, hands on healing, communication of knowledge, caring and nurturing, teaching and instruction, and just knowing that someone is there if you need them. Always come from a place of love and understanding because there can be no change, no advancement, no joy and no true connection without it. When you understand the true power of love you must spread it far and wide.

Thank-you Father Benedict.

What's Really Going on?

The whole world seems to revolve around sex, or so it appears, but that's only half the story. Everybody seems to be doing it, looking for it, or at least talking about it, but underneath this animalistic approach is a longing for contact, connection and love and that is what's really going on. From the time you are born into the world of matter until you depart from it, you are all looking for that feeling of bonding and belonging to something that is embedded into your very soul, it's a longing to feel connection once again to the source energy from which you came. It may at first seem that everyone has sex on their mind but that's just the tip of the ice berg, what lies beneath is the real reason and that's what people are unconsciously searching for, of course the actual act itself is extremely pleasurable especially when it's given and received with love and caring, two people exchanging energy can be closer to the source when their energies are combined, not many people will recognise this so a person who has a lot of sexual activity or partners obviously has a very strong urge to connect and this act will help them to do so. Of course, this is not the only way to connect but it is one way. It is sad when within a long-term relationship this act is no longer an option, because not only is it healthy for the spirit its healthy for the body too, it keeps the blood circulating, the heart pumping, the limbs flexible and the whole body in a happy state. What does lie beneath the water under the tip of the ice berg is a search for love, to feel it and to give it because to feel connected to a partner is to feel connected to all that is, and this my friends is what everybody wants. It's as if you are all salmon, having lived your life you are now swimming back up stream against the strong current to try to get back home, it's a struggle but you swim and you strive to get there because you have to get back to the source of where all life began, so you may start the whole process over again.

Thank-you Father Benedict.

Honeycombs

Today I find myself inside a barn watching two of the Fathers extracting honey from the combs. They're spinning it in a wooden barrel by turning the handle very quickly and therefore releasing the honey from where it was deposited.

Knowledge

Anything you come across is never new, it's something you will vaguely remember or something you re-learn, usually given via a friend, media, or spiritually, you then put your twist on it and call it your own. It's all recycled information because there is nothing new, the truth is the truth and you can't change that, you can only make it fit the occasion for which it's needed. Do not be annoyed if someone "steals" your idea's because basically they weren't yours to start with, some people are short sighted and some long sighted, that's to say some cast their nets far, have a good imagination and are able to put a creative twist on their projects, and some simply can't be bothered to put time or effort into their creations, and then take your twist and claim the whole thing as their own. Instead of being upset or hurt by their actions because that's the ego talking, you should be pleased that your twist has been used again.

Help everyone to see their own potential, it's easy when helping a child to grow, you are patient and giving of your time, for example tying a shoelace, again and again you show them until they get it and are pleased with their efforts, but somehow you feel different when people get older or you don't show them, and they copy what they have seen you do but there's no difference really, the child copies and that's ok the adult copies and that's somehow wrong, why? Perhaps it's because one is given and the other is taken, but in the grand scheme of things it's all information and there to be shared. It's no different with knowledge, if you are able to process things quickly and clearly it's your job to pass it onto others, because all information is there to be shared and not to be kept to yourself, if you need to break it down and simplify it so they may make sense of it as with the shoelace example then do so. Just because you have gone out of your way to gain the knowledge to help and assist in a happy life you can't think it's exclusively yours, change the format if you must, and realise not everyone is blessed with a quick mind. There are lots of different levels of advancement, old souls learn quicker because of experience and young souls don't so they will need help. Everyone has gifts and talents to share and everything needs to be in the flow of creation, if the flow in is halted then so is the flow out, it's like a tank of water, how can it remain fresh if its left, undisturbed it becomes stagnant and old, the old (ideas) water needs to be removed and topped up with fresh new water every day, in order to keep it alive and full of oxygen, sometimes things do become undisturbed and stagnant, the beliefs you have held onto for so long are now being challenged and this makes you feel uncomfortable, but be brave replace the old with the new and as ever continue forward.

Thank-you Father Benedict.

Karma

In this life you get away with nothing. You may secretly praise yourself and think you're clever with your decisions and actions, you may tell yourself that its ok it doesn't matter and make up all sorts of excuses for your behaviour, when in truth the only person who's eyes you are pulling the wool over are your own. Maybe at the time of your deceit which obviously can include any number of things, you will be congratulating yourself on a job well done, but at some point, later the truth will hit you and you'll realise just how much your past actions effect what is happening to you right now. You are all looking for love and that's the reason anyone does anything, the need to be recognised and loved but the only way it can be lasting is when it's done in the right way otherwise it will always be thwarted with grief. You may be so blinded by the way you are living that it begins to feel normal, and you don't even question your actions anymore because you have such a strong need for love and acknowledgement, but if you were mindful you would realise that every action has a reaction, this is true karma, for no one without exception gets away with anything. It's not crime and punishment or retribution as a lot of people believe, it is the natural order of things, and when you finally see this you will know that it's time for a change. You can begin firstly, by changing your thoughts and when you do this a lot of other things will automatically fall into place. It's the ego that puts a lot of distorted thoughts into your head, you're a good person so reward yourself with this, or go ahead and treat yourself with that, you deserve it, and in most cases you are a good person but always be honest, and only reward yourself if it's not at the expense of another. No one has the right to inflict any kind of pain, humility, anger or bullying to get what they need, and even if it does go unnoticed by others, it will still be out there in the universe, what's done can't be undone but it can be stopped. The recipe for love is only give out what you want to receive, it's that simple.

Thank-you Father Benedict.

A Perfect Day

Today I find myself on our bench in the warm sunshine, the sky is blue and cloudless, there are beautiful flowers nodding their heads in the soft breeze's, butterflies and bees are chasing around, you could not find a more perfect day.

D = Detach

In order to move forward successfully with life there is a need to learn to detach oneself emotionally from everything. That doesn't mean becoming emotionally unattached to others or the self because love and compassion are essential to a fulfilling life, it means observing all with a calm logic as if it were happening to someone else. Life is full of contradictions that are sometimes hard to work out. Once you understand, accept and try to detach from taking everything so personally or emotionally you are ready to heal in all ways, physically and mentally. Whenever you feel injustice at some one's words or actions remember this is the way they perceive the world and the things that make it go around, constantly being resentful or angry with any one for being who they are isn't fair on them or you, because toxic thoughts bring about a toxic body. It shouldn't matter what people do to you or think about you, whether it's their intention to hurt or to heal, or to simply try to get you to see their point of view, it's their karma, how you receive it and more importantly how you feel about it, is yours. What you do about it is also very important because revenge is never justified, even if you believe it to be so, never try to ease your conscience by making excuses for your actions, that's the work of the ego. You may ask the question, if I'm detached and don't react when someone does something off to me, will they think it's ok to do it again because I'm an easy target? No, not so, do not allow their thinking to penetrate you, you are stronger than that, you will simply remove yourself temporarily or permanently, you do not need to argue about it you just stay clear until the upset is over. At some point it should start to become apparent to them that unkind words do not get what they require, and another approach is needed, people respond to kindness and not aggression. Seeing things from your new perspective does not make you a "Mr Spock", someone who is logical with no humane feelings, you can still be very loving, caring and emotional to yourself and to others when the time is right to do so, but not injecting it into situations that doesn't call for it so be realistic and don't make a drama out of nothing. Feeling hurt and having the need to do something about it in actual terms or just thoughts are more harmful to yourself than to others, so let it pass you by because no one can have an argument with themselves, it always takes two. Start each day afresh and with love in your heart and a smile on your face.

Thank- you Father Benedict.

Experience

You need to experience all life has to offer to make it real for you. Example, you can tell a child that the radiator is hot don't touch it, and for a while he will do as you say, but to make it real for him he will at some point put his hand on it so he can make sense of what you say, you cannot fully explain to him or anyone how something feels because feelings are personal. You may say time and time again don't run, walk, look where you are going, and he will for a while listen but because he has so much natural energy inside with no particular outlet for it yet, he feels the need to run everywhere without considering the consequences of his actions, that's to say until he goes headlong into a nasty fall which obviously hurts and then makes him think twice, for a while. There is no difference between the child body and the child spirit, you may have the appearance of an older physical body, but you may still be a spiritual toddler, and will need to experience life to gain your own perspective. Wisdom cannot be fully understood unless it's experienced, and that is another reason you come to earth school to experience the experience itself. People must go headlong into situations and lessons to gain understanding, knowledge and finally wisdom. On a deeper level, that of soul level there is an understanding that all good and bad must be experienced to be able to move forward with your journey. To be told and not experienced is only half of the understanding and half of the wisdom. With each lesson it is right to pass that knowledge onto others so they may know it, but it only becomes their wisdom when it's experienced first- hand for this gives it a whole deeper truth and depth. You'll find that in helping others along their way you are also helping yourself, because when we Guides see you helping others with no thought of return for yourself, it opens the doorway for us to help you even more, we will bring many more opportunities for growth to you, and in doing this we will be helping ourselves to grow also, each act of kindness and service is growth for all those concerned.

Thank-you Father Benedict, what a lovely explanation.

A Busy, Happy Life

I find myself inside a small court-yard, this is somewhere I haven't been before, it seems that although the island it is quite small there is so much that I still haven't seen. Two of the Brothers are chopping wood for the fires, I watch them as they go about their tasks laughing and joking together. It's so much nicer to do your work with a smile on your face. A happy positive person equals a happy positive life.

For any true healing to take place the mind, body and spirit must be in harmony as one. Each of you needs love and acceptance from family and friends but most forget or are unaware that self love is probably even more important.

Every dis-ease starts in the mind and the gut, sending signals to one another, if the gut is happy the mind will be and vice versa, whether the dis-ease is illness, joint pain, broken bones, blood disorders or respiratory problems, they will have all started here, and are termed as psychosomatic, which doesn't mean it's in the mind and therefore doesn't exist, but that it started in the mind because of low self-esteem, an unhappy mind equals and unhappy body. It also works in reverse, everyone has so much to be grateful for and if they recognise this fact, psychosomatically they will bring about a happy, healthy and contented life. Unfortunately, not a lot of people are yet aware of these facts and they don't seem to be able to connect the dots, they think it's just their bad luck that they have become ill or out of action.

Thank-you Father Benedict.

Busy Lives

The Fathers lead such busy lives, when they are not at their prayers, they have so many important jobs to do, care for their animals, fish to catch, bees to keep, food to grow and to prepare, cloth to spin and for some, words to record on parchment. But in all there must be a balance, rest and play. A balance of energies is needed in all aspects of life to keep it running smoothly.

Masculine and Feminine
The whole of life consists of opposites, and they need to be in balance to run smoothly, unfortunately your world at this moment is not exactly as balanced as it should be. The male and female energies need to be corrected, both are obviously needed, the male energy is strong, dependable, practical and functional, whereas the female energy is caring, loving, nurturing and accepting, and the two need each other to function and to compliment, it doesn't work if one is more apparent than the other. Earth at this moment is quite heavily in the corner of the masculine, whereas back in the 1960's there was a lot more feminine energy to be found and felt, there was every day talk of love and much consideration for the fellow man, and a lot of this came from an unexpected source, war. The Vietnam war was probably one of the first times the male population questioned the decision to go to war, before this time it was looked upon as something to be proud of, an honour to die for your cause or your country, but these enlightened young men started to look at things in a different way, from a female perspective. There was a lot more female energy contained within them, a softer loving energy to blend with their masculine ones. One needs the other to survive, unfortunately since that time the balance has slowly moved back in favour of the masculine. For anything to survive and thrive it needs to be nurtured, loved and cared for to find its balance again, one fine example is that of earth, it's not known as Mother Earth without good reason, it needs feminine energy and does not respond well to the dominance of the male energies. This does not mean men and women per-say, because all contain a mix

of both energies, it means that there is a lot more aggression and assertiveness in both, and not so much softer feminine ones. A lot of people are tending to think more about themselves than others, there is a lot of aggression when for example driving on the road, when trying to put your own point of view across, or simply wanting things right now in a demanding way. Obviously, there are times when you will need to stand up for yourself against the bullies or the cruel and dominant people, but by far the best way is that of the female approach with love and consideration, because there is no one or nothing that doesn't respond to love and kindness.

Thank-you Father Benedict.

The Natural Order

Sometimes I ask Father Benedict: What's beneficial for me to know today please?

Answer: To be patient and tolerant of all things.

Everything happens at the precise time it's meant to, and there is a natural order to everything in the universe, if you try to change things you won't see the best outcome. Seeds take their time to germinate and grow, all the conditions must be right, the temperature, the water and the light all play their part. A baby will take the right amount of time to grow and mature in the womb, it needs the Mother to eat healthily and drink plenty of fresh water to produce the perfect child. Day follows night as surely it must, and life, death and rebirth is the natural order of the universe. It is however hard to come to terms with, when you lose someone you love, you will probably feel they were taken from you too quickly, you are angry and sad, but again this is the natural order of grieving, sadness, despair, anger and finally acceptance, and quite often these feelings are as much about you as the loved one who has passed. The sadness, you cry for their loss in your life, of the big hole they have left behind, the fact that you can no longer sit and chat, or ask for their advice, and you miss the very presence of them, their arms around you. The anger you feel, you tell yourself that if you had departed first you wouldn't have had to deal with such a dept of emotion, feeling their loss and just knowing that there is not a thing you can do to change it, the despair, you have cried a thousand tears and are exhausted, and you wish with all your heart you could wake up and find everything the same as it had always been, and finally the acceptance, as you come to terms with the fact that whatever emotion you experience nothing changes. This is how it is. This is the natural order of things. You will then begin to realise that nothing does change; the love you always shared is still there and sometimes felt even stronger, it doesn't finish with physical separation, love is forever and once it's given it exists as a vibration in the universe now and forever more. That depth of love will of course wax and wane as it does, not unlike the moon, sometimes it will be glowing and light up the whole of your world and at other times it will be shining quietly in the background, ready to burst open when you need a blast to make you smile again. Love like the pain of loss will find its own level, to feel both with such power when it's new, raw and filled with emotion is over bearing, and no one could sustain this level for any length of time. The human mind, body and spirit will deal with each at the level of understanding they have reached at this point on their path, because you simply cannot absorb any more comfortably, it would be power overload and the whole circuit would explode. All things find their natural order, and this is just how it is, so to try to change things would benefit no one, least of all you.

Thank-you Father Benedict.

Springtime

Every time I land on the island I never know where I will be, or what season I will find myself in. I look around and see it's Spring, I see primroses and bluebells amongst the trees, which are bright green, all is looking healthy and fresh and makes me smile, I think I like Springtime best with its promise of good things to come.

Father Benedict Tells Me Everyone Has a Need to be Seen
By that, I mean a need to be recognised and appreciated for the wonderful human beings that you are. Everyone has a need to be heard also, this is not the ego but a basic need to know that you matter in the world, and if sadly this was missing in your early year's then part of you will be forever searching. Of course, parents and carers all have busy lives, caring, guiding and nurturing, it takes a lot of energy to be a Mum or a Dad, but time should be divided up fairly, children's time in the day and parent's time when they're asleep. It's so important to be a good role model for the young ones and even more so to make them feel seen, acknowledged and feel safe and loved. It's no good trying to push your longings or ambitions onto them, because they are not you and will have their own ideas of careers and past times, yet so many times youngsters are expected to follow the family traditions regarding career choices and this doesn't always work, because each must tread their own path and be seen to do so. Never neglect them for your own pursuits, spend as much time together as you can, because you will never get that time back again, watching you and how you interact with them is how they learn to be good parents themselves. If a parent is absent it will affect the little ones, and even more so if they share a house and are absent emotionally, there is nothing more upsetting than someone who is indifferent to another family member, whether intentional or not. Indifference is a very harmful emotion to give out or to deal with especially if you claim to care about them. Love needs expression. If children are made to feel invisible they will carry this with them into adulthood, and either replicate it in

their choice of partner because it somehow feels strangely comfortable, or if they have been able to recognise the indifference and lack of connection and will happily now choose a more suitable partner who is different in every way from what they experienced, and be a very attentive loving but fair parent. If for example your parent had a busy social life with not a lot of time for you, you may find yourself repeating this pattern still in the hope that you will be seen by them, even if it's as a chip off the old block, he/she is so popular and has such a lot of friends just like me, but at what cost? Your children won't see you, any more than you saw your absent parent, history will be repeating itself. Or are you further down your path now and can remember how it felt, how sad you were when once again you were told "I'd love to stay and play but I just have to pop out for a while", or "we'll do that tomorrow, I promise", but you learnt too quickly that tomorrow never comes. Feel pleased and honoured that your partner and children want to spend time with you, because you only get back what you give out, life is a mirror and if you don't put the love, care and connection in place now later on in your life when you are the one who's asking, they will certainly be a chip off the block then and tell you, "tomorrow, I promise"!

Thank-you Father Benedict.

Self-Love

To love another, you must first have respect for yourselves, you need to be at peace in your own hearts and have love for the self, obviously, that does not mean ego, being conceited or vain, it means being quietly confident. Within the daily lives of all there will be times of disagreement and upsets this is normal, but if someone is willing to put up with continual bad, selfish or cruel behaviour you can be assured that self -love and self- respect is missing. If you find that you are agreeing to certain behaviours or attitudes that aren't yours, and do not feel right to you, you are not being very kind to yourself or the other person involved. Neither of you will grow as people if one gives aggression or inflicts pain, by word or deed and the other is willing to put up with it because of lack of confidence and worth, this will inevitably push you both further apart and back on your spiritual path. You may try to reason with yourself and think I can't have everything in life, my partner works hard and provides a roof over my head, I never have to worry about the bills, and I get to have lovely holidays so if he does stay a little too long after work, out drinking and unwinding with the boys that's a small price to pay, or, my wife/partner is cold and distant these days and isn't interested in making love together any more, I can even feel her recoil from my touch which makes me very sad, but that's okay because she is a wonderful mother and wife and she manages the house and the kids so well, I don't know what I would do without her. But if you stop to consider these things are you being fair to yourself when you are sad and crying out for love and affection. Do you feel lost, do you keep quiet because voicing your desires makes you look needy or have you tried and gotten no response, but they are important to you because they are what you need at this time to feel whole, you are unfulfilled, incomplete and lacking in self-care. If you loved yourself as you love your parents and your children you would not stand by and watch someone slowly destroy them, you would step in, voice your opinions and stand up for them because you would not want them to feel so hurt or abused. It's no difference with self-love or self-respect, if you want to grow and want the people who share your life to grow, you must be aware and be mindful of karmic debt, either do it now or do it the next time it's your choice. Please put a value on your happiness and don't settle for anything that doesn't hit your truth or make you happy.

Thank-you Father Benedict.

A North Wind

Today our Island is being blown about by a chilly north wind, as I look out to sea the waves have a white foam top to them, seals are ducking and diving in and out having fun. The air is very cold so Father Benedict and I make our way to one of the little fishing huts, which is nice as we haven't been here for a while. I have a question today please, I say as we sit ourselves down on an old crate, warm now that we're out of the wind.

Reincarnation
Question: *If we all reincarnate so that we may experience everything life has to offer, then why don't we remember anything about our previous lives?*

Answer: One of the main reasons would be because it would be far too complicated for the average person to deal with, for example, as you know people exist within soul groups that enter and exit many times in different roles in the play that you know as life. Your Mother could change roles making her your child, or your Father may enter as your Grandson this time, perhaps because of some unfinished family business, you may have experienced a very close loving relationship with him as the Father, who cared for and was always there for you, and it was your dearest wish to do the same for him in his elder years, but you never got the chance because in your eyes he passed too soon, so for among other reasons he now comes to you in a different overcoat, so you can fulfil your wish. But just think how complicated that could make life if you remembered all of this.

Another reason is life's lessons and tasks, which in some cases may be of benefit to you if you did remember, perhaps you were given an important lesson which you didn't handle very well and this fact played on your mind for the rest of your life, through loss of concentration you caused a road traffic accident and a painful passing for someone, If you wanted, you could repeat a similar scenario under different circumstances, maybe a boating incident and through your quick thinking this time you did save the day, it would be helpful but also very complicated.

I have also talked before about child prodigies and the fact that they are carrying on unconsciously from the point where they had left off, this too could prove to be confusing if one remembered. Another fine example is déjà- vu, the feeling you've seen or been there before, some do get a glimpse of another life in another time and place, and of past lives but they're usually fleeting and disjointed and sometimes a bit upsetting.

In the example of the Mother /Daughter relationship if you both remembered your experience together, and if your Mother had abused you in some way, was neglectful, a bully, or unloving this may be the perfect chance for you to give her a taste of her own medicine! You can see how it just wouldn't work, no room for advancement here, it would only mean a lifetime's worth of missed opportunities. Each incarnation must be a fresh start and a chance to do the best you can with the new, or not so tasks and players.

Thank-you Father Benedict.

The Island

The causeway is completely open, a perfect crossing to the island. It's a bright sunny day and warm for the time of year, it's autumn and the leaves on the trees are turning lovely shades of golden, yellow and red. Father Benedict is waiting for me with two baskets, ones we had made ourselves previously, they have a divider down the middle, one half for any fruit, nuts and berries we come across to eat, and the other half is for things we can't, but are used to heal. Over his shoulder he carries two sacks, which he explains are for collecting the decorations we will use for the chapel. We go into a small coppice of trees and there we put blackberries into our baskets first, there are a few berries I don't recognise, but then we find some elderberries, which I know as I use them myself to make a vitamin c syrup, the collection on the other side are all things that I don't know, berries, leaves, fungi, and small pieces of bark, all for healing purposes. By now we have filled our sacks also with willow, conkers, acorns and other pretty things, we then head back to the chapel to decorate, I realise at this point it's harvest and that's the reason for this excursion, to gather and bring inside so we may give thanks and blessings for all that nature provides. As we work Father Benedict tells me there is to be a harvest supper tonight, which will consist of a stew of vegetables and mutton, the animal which is to used is no longer of an age to bear any more young, she has lived a wonderful carefree life outside in the sunshine and fresh air, and has given birth to a number of healthy young, she's been a perfect Mother. Now in the chain of events that makes up her life she is to be blessed, revered and thanked in a service in the chapel for all she has given, she is then to be used in the time-honoured way to nourish and to sustain life. Thanks be to her and all wonderful creatures. We continue to decorate the chapel now in silence and thought. Life marches on and time stands still for no one. It is right that one is born lives and then returns to the place from which he came, it's the same for man and beast.

Thank-you Father Benedict.

Respect and Honour All Life

The best way to respect a human life well lived, is to honour the passing and keep the memory of that person alive with fond words for they are gone from sight only. You are lucky to live in the age of photographs and images as this helps to keep them alive for you, but more than that, you can make a stronger connection with your loved ones when you look into their eyes in the photo, and with practice you will recognise their vibration (the feeling of them) and you will know that you are again sharing time together, all be it in a different form now. Keep your family alive to your children and grandchildren with tales of their adventures, and words and phrases they used. Laugh with fondness as you remember the Christmases and special occasions you shared, talk about your childhood and the things you all got up to together and the fun you had, for as long as you talk about them you make them real to your family, and keep them alive so their energies will be felt by all. Acknowledge their struggles and hardships and know they experienced them, so you didn't have to, this is tribe or family karma, once dealt with it doesn't have to be repeated, (different to personal karma). Thank them also for their guidance and their love which is unconditional and something they continue to give, be open to all the little signs that come to as this is how they communicate now. Speak to them often for reassurance and ask for their guidance when you have an important decision to make, you will get an answer, just in a different way now, look for feathers, coins, a song, a familiar scent or fragrance, an advert on the television for their favourite tipple or holiday destination, type of car they drove, if you're open minded you will recognise it. Love never dies, it's just not possible, the flesh has a time span, and the soul does not. It is of course very sad for the earth family to be parted physically from their loved one, nobody could ever deny that but once you have the precious knowledge that it's only physically the pain becomes less and a little easier to bear. Parting is never easy, but reunions are wonderful.

Thank-you Father Benedict.

The Monastery Grounds

Father Benedict and I are walking on the edge of the monastery grounds and out into the woods. It's Autumn and the leaves are turning lovely shades of red, amber and gold, Father tells me some people feel sad when summer has come to an end and Winter is on the way, but Winter is a time for rest and reflection, a time to think about what you may do next Summer, and how you may use your time a little differently to make the most of the daylight hours. Life like time is everlasting, everything comes back, as you sow so shall you reap, so it is up to you to make it the best summer you can by careful thought and forward planning now.

Feelings
Changing your life is a feeling and not something you just say you are going to do. You must agree with yourself, if I'm going to change I must now realise that my lack of wisdom and knowledge has led me to the place I find myself in at this precise moment, I fully accept this is because of my past thoughts, words and actions, which at times could have been better and at other times were very off track, so I now make better choices. If I'm going to really live, I give a hundred per cent to myself, to others and any situation I find myself in, to give any less will only give me a percentage of anything back. Attitude's and understanding are what's required, and you must accept that what you give you will get back. It is easy to bring about a change with feelings, which are the guide to how your life is really going, and they are the clue to everything you experience, the unseen is more accurate than what you see with your eyes as they can distort your vision. Example, before you is standing a very beautiful overcoat but not a beautiful soul, giving the illusion of a person who has your best interest at heart, but these clever people know how to flatter the ego, and because everyone has one they like to believe what they hear, put feelings into the experience and you will find it takes on a whole new meaning, don't look at life but feel it and it will take on a whole new depth. Don't just say I love you in response to someone else's I love you, have the feelings present before you

say it. Open your heart to compassion and feel another's plight as if it were your own, that way you are far more inclined to do something about it. Don't just empathise, have the power within you to change lives because you have a duty to yourself and others to help everyone have a good life. Everyone is looking for the same thing and that of course is love and it's the best feeling there is, to have it and to give it.

Thank-you Father Benedict.

In Chains

While you judge, compare and criticise you hold yourselves in chains and are not free to see the beauty of everything that surrounds you. You all desperately want a happy and contented life, but a lot go about it in the wrong way. People and situations come in and out of your life for a reason, to help you to grow and mature spiritually, some people stay for a lifetime and some don't, some will stay for many lifetimes or until you have worked through the lessons successfully and all that remains for each other is love. Some will enter quickly and leave the same way, because either the lesson is a quick one or there's not a lot of depth to what needs to be learnt, whatever the case, leave no room for judgement. Do not chain yourself to the illusion, for most of what you see isn't real, people will act out their lives based on what they perceive as right, and many arguments have been fought over basically nothing at all, which is all that's left once the fighting has finished. To judge, compare or be in competition with anyone is quite a pointless exercise for it doesn't matter who's the quickest, the smartest or the prettiest because these things are just the superficial work of the ego and the fastest way to tie yourself in knots, just be content with what you have and who you are, be quietly confident and this alone will give your spirit time to shine instead of time wasted. Don't chain yourself to your ego because this only causes upset and judgement. Be yourself because you are a beautiful soul who has much to give to the world in your own particular way, be an individual and don't follow the crowd just to fit in, be your own shining light and others will want to be near you, be a trendsetter not a trend- follower, be free to fly and don't feel the need to conform to the opinion of others, for this is the way to move forward along your path. When you choose to be yourself and not a carbon copy of everyone else your light will shine bright and this will attract to you all you need, like moths to your flame. You attract to you all you hold inside so if that's judgement and criticism people will judge and criticise you, but if it's love, admiration and understanding that's what you'll receive.

Thank-you Father Benedict.

Karma and Sugar

Sugar is the scourge of the modern world and if not recognised as such and treated in accordance with the laws of the universe, it will destroy so much of mankind. If you will it's pay-back time for ill-gotten gains. How many lives were destroyed, how many families torn apart and how many people oppressed for the sake of it. Greed was the nature of the slave trade and sugar was at the heart of it. White gold. It poisoned the minds of the men who pursued it and now it poisons the minds of those who are helplessly addicted to it. Anything that is gotten by force or cruelty is never going to have a happy outcome. Karma. It may take a day it may take a year, or it may take a hundred years, but you can be sure that every action will have a reaction. Tobacco and sugar, both ill-gotten, and both are now finding their karmic dept. Both destroying families and hopes for the future. What makes someone think they can steel or take anything that's not theirs to take, let alone a human life, how mind-blind, how cruel and heartless, and now the world is paying for their greed. Tobacco is a choice but once tried a few times becomes the master and you the slave, a slave to your addiction. Sugar is also a choice but in these modern times it very cleverly finds its way into almost all food that today's people enjoy, so it too becomes the master. Sugar helps to destroy the body by depleting the good bacteria and the immune system, it piles on the pounds and helps to create an overweight unhealthy world that's sick and getting sicker every day. Of course, you can't change your past as those were your choices then but today you can create your future by the choices you make now, you are all human it's true but please take some responsibility for the gift of the body you find yourselves in. Show a good example to your children, it's not about having it all, that's greed, it's about everything in moderation, how many keep sugar for a treat? Not many, and if you indulge one day do you wait a while before doing it again. As your good bacteria gets destroyed and replaced by the bad your choices become less and less as they take over your body, your will power decreases until you have no choice at all in the foods you feed your body temple, fast foods, soda pop, sweets, cake, and chocolate, modern bread even has a sugar coating on it. You owe it to future generations to be able to run, jump and play, to be fit and healthy and don't forget about reincarnation, which everyone will experience again and again, so you owe it to yourself as well. Why lead a life where you are constantly tired, ill, anxious or depressed, when by just a few good choices like fruit and vegetables and living simply you can have a brilliant life experience.

Thank-you Father Benedict.

Walking with Father Benedict

Today I find myself walking with Father Benedict, across the small stone bridge where my family line up on either side, it's so lovely to see them all and I can feel their loving energy as I pass between them. As I take steps along my personal pathway, I like everyone feel a little drained, sad or just out of sorts at times, and when this happens, they understand and can feel my lack of energy and that's the reason they are here today, to give me a loving boost of their energies. I stand for a while in the middle and absorb them all and thank them for being near in times of need just as they would be if they still had their earthly overcoats on.

A question please: Why, do we place ourselves under so much pressure?

Answer: A good question, why do you place such heavy burdens upon yourselves, I must do this, that can't wait, I need to look as if I'm totally in control of every little thing in my life. Well you don't! It is perfectly OK to say to yourself and others, I'm struggling, I'm tired, I can't cope, no one is going to judge you, at least no one who cares about you. It's perfectly normal to admit you're finding things difficult, everyone has times when it all gets too much, but if anyone asks how you are the immediate response is always "yes I'm fine thanks, how are you" and the answer to that will be yes me too! It's a shame people can't be a little more open and honest especially to close friends and family, but you don't because you don't want to make others feel uncomfortable or feel under pressure to come up with a solution, but if people were honest and shared their true feelings it would open the door for others to do the same, denying your feelings and pushing them to the back of your mind isn't helpful to your health or well-being. I do not mean for you to be negative and dwell on the bad times or go into long explanations about private matters, but it's fine to say "I'm having a bit of a tough time just now so please excuse me if I don't feel like chatting today", please do this especially at times of sadness or loss when you should be honest about your grief. You need to acknowledge to yourself and others how you are feeling so it can help you to move past what has caused it. Healing can be a lengthy process depending on the severity of it, so don't put a sticking plaster on it and hope it will go away, because at some point you will have to pull it off and that will hurt even more. Cry, tears are a great healer and they're there for a good reason, to wash away the pain, it's not a sign of weakness, men in general think this way, but it is in fact a sign of great strength, if more little boys were taught to share their feelings and cry there wouldn't be so much silent sorrow in their hearts. Men, women, girls and boys all the same flesh and blood, with the same love and feelings. Fathers should be encouraging their sons to shed their tears at unhappy times; it's a very liberating thing to share in. Don't smile and say I'm fine when you are breaking up inside, let it go and find peace in doing so. Don't give yourself a time limit, it will take as long as it takes, moving on and change is the nature of life but by properly acknowledging and dealing with things when they happen, will better prepare you to help others with similar experiences, you are all on earth to help yourself and others, life is a gentle unfolding with all sorts of things to deal with and to enjoy.

Thank-you Father Benedict.

A Mirror

Whoever you are with and at whatever stage your relationship is at, it is a mirror of what you are inside, your view of the world, childhood experiences, friends, lovers will have all played a part. You spend your time looking for romantic love when in truth that doesn't last very long at all, but it does get replaced by something more meaningful and lasting. A lot of people can't get past the euphoria of the first part of love, the thrill, where you can't keep your hands off each other, but when this quietens down and makes way for the real stuff to come in, they think maybe this person isn't the right one after all, or they can't or don't want to wait for the real love to develop. Some rush in so quickly they never get the chance to know the person or their personality, there has to be more to any relationship than the physical, that's just a part of it, of course two people have to be compatible here but there has to be other factors as well, their likes, dislikes, their expectations of each other, how kind and caring, how compassionate and thoughtful all play a part. If the physical is great but the other aspects are a struggle, then the relationship won't progress very far, and discontentment will creep in. You cannot be with someone just because they show you some attention, this is the mirror showing you that there are things that you need to address within your own life first, you may have a distorted vision of yourself and come to believe that you're unattractive or unlovable, have no confidence or self- esteem because of your past experiences, perhaps you didn't get picked for team games at school, or you didn't get that valentine card, so you settle for a relationship that's not quite right, you are then attracting another person who also believes there is something not quite right with them, you both unconsciously are that little stray dog who once it gets a friendly pat on the head follows you home. Once you can begin to see that there's nothing wrong with either of you, you immediately start to raise your vibrations and the parts that aren't working will simply fade away or you won't notice them anymore, the only way to change any situation is by loving what you already have, and this in turn makes way to have more of what you love.

Thank you, Father Benedict.

A Question

When we meet up, I simply ask Father Benedict,

What words of wisdom do you have for me to pass on today please?

Why, When You Are All Seeking Happiness, Do You Create Misery Instead?

I hear lots of people say I just want to be happy; so if this is true what goes wrong. Attitude, selfishness, greed, thoughtless actions and a whole host of other things, so what can be done about it?

Happiness is a state of mind, it's not something you can buy or pretend to be, it's something that occurs without effort or conscious thought, it is peace, contentment and a calm mind, and without these things in place it will forever elude you. Accepting all that has happened to you without judgement or blame and coming to the realisation that all events are there for your growth. Everyone wants to be happy but so many go about it in the wrong way, I'm hurt so I'll let the world know about it, it's my right and I want it now, I'm scared so I'll put up my barriers.

People very often carry their set of problems or lessons from one relationship to another, never dealing with them properly and hoping with a change of partner things will be different, but they seldom are, because it's themselves that need to recognise the pattern and the lesson contained within, it needs to be dealt with, and so with a different attitude to life and the people around them it's safe to move forward. You will attract to you like a magnet, the people who will try to get you to see your lesson over and over, until you do see it and can leave it behind you for good, leaving you to then enjoy a loving and peaceful life. It's never easy to change a lifetime's habits and points of view, but if you want to find contentment it must be done.

Thank-you Father Benedict.

A Walled Garden

Today I find myself in the lovely walled garden, so peaceful calm and warm, it's been a long time since I've been here and it's lovely to be back. All the produce for the kitchen is grown along with lots of herbs for flavouring, and for healing the body.

Healing
Any illness that occurs in the body will have started within the spirit; you may consider the spirit to be the self-esteem if that makes more sense for you. The mind body and spirit/self-esteem must all be in balance and harmony with each other for good mental and physical health. If the body is fine but the spirit is low for any reason this can be the trigger it needs to set about a disease, spelt this way to emphasize the body being dis-at-ease with itself and/or the mind. Everyone needs love and acceptance from family and friends, but most forget that acceptance of the self is just as important, if not more so. You compare yourselves to others and try to measure up to their ideals which is silly because what's right for them can never be right for you.

An example of this, siblings, there were three children who were loved and cared for equally by their parents and all had their own unique personalities and gifts, one had the gift of a quick mind, the ability to add up a column of numbers at speed, and was able to spell the most difficult words from a young age, this is indeed a bright child. The second child was extremely clever with their hands, could sew, knit, cook, bake and create beautiful works of art, however the youngest child struggled with all of these things and felt inadequate, I'm just stupid she thought sadly, but what she failed to understand is, her gift wasn't a visual one, but equally important, her gift was that of love and compassion, which incidentally wasn't so strong in the other two. She was the first one there when either of the others was upset, she was the one who checked on the elderly neighbours, fed and loved any stray animals she came across, and the first to look after their own parents when they are old and unable. She measured herself against the visible and was often angry and depressed because she

86

thought she was inadequate, and didn't like herself very much, so the spirit inside was sad, lost and alone, she didn't see the beautiful loving person that dwelt within, and so began the tiny seeds of disharmony which in turn led over many years, to dis-ease. But wait a moment this is now something that makes her feel special and unique, she has manifested a something that she can focus upon, a something that makes her stand out from the other two, they don't have a dis-ease! At last she is special too. Unfortunately for her she will carry this forever unless she can be at ease with herself and put aside the dis-harmony which is in her own mind, it's a sad fact that we can't always see our own worth but other people's stand out to us. Strangely enough her two sisters would have liked to be more kind and caring but couldn't be bothered to put in the effort. Change the thoughts and change the life. Every dis-ease starts in the mind of the person.

Thank-you Father Benedict: very insightful.

Filling Baskets

Father Benedict and I are filling our baskets with the produce from the garden. We pull up carrots, parsnips, onions, and cabbage, these will go into the pot along with chicken and seaweed which is used to flavour, it then slowly cooks all day. It's quite a task because the Fathers and Brothers are always hungry after their busy day, so we need to gather a lot.

As we work, he asks me, "Have you ever wondered about your name?"

Did you know you chose your name, or rather the vibration of it before you came to the earth in the flesh; it carries the vibration of your soul within it and is as unique as your fingerprint. You may have heard some expectant Mothers say I have a few names but I'll know for sure when I see my baby which one is right, and this is correct as she will pick up unconsciously a vibration that is very similar to her own at this time, the two vibrations will change over the years as the child develops its own personality but at this stage they will be very closely linked. It feels nice when your name is used especially when used in a loving context for example when making love, when it's spoken, you'll find it resonates with your soul, but the reverse is also true when used in anger, words hurt, and this is multiplied with the use of your name. Your family name has the same value to it, and this is one reason why a lot of women are reluctant to leave it behind when they marry, so they will keep their tribal name and add the new name on the end. It's important to belong and it's something to be proud of, one reason for a family coat of arms or an emblem on any team shirt, a sense of belonging to something special. Children who are adopted have such a need to find out about their roots, they need family connections and ties to make sense of their lives, backgrounds are researched for family trees and ancestor's, there is a strong need for them to know and to connect to something bigger than themselves, it's not just for the curiosity aspect.

Thank-you Father Benedict.

Don't Fear Death

Most people upon the earth plane fear death, they don't talk about it and few prepare themselves for it even though they know it's inevitable, as you say there are only two things in life which are guaranteed, death and taxes! On some level we understand your fear, it's not death per-say but the fear and upset of parting from your loving family, but have faith and know for sure that yes, while some do go on ahead of you, you are never separate from each other in the true sense of the word. Each night while you are "sleeping" you are together, and each day they stand beside you watching over you and trying their best to get your attention to guide and help you along your pathway. To be perfectly honest when you stand this side of the glass and watch the struggles that befall so many, it's then you should be in fear, fear of earth life. Life here is so much less complicated, no pretence, no point, as we have the ability to see all, no point in saying one thing and meaning another, no diets! No hunger because a body needs food, while a spirit needs feeding in a different way, that of experience, knowledge and wisdom. No heat to contend with, no cold, no drought or no flood, what you find here is perfection on every level. As your awareness and wisdom increases you will find yourself dwelling on a higher level, dimension or plane of existence, love is what counts here so never fear that you'll be in the company of less warm-hearted souls or indeed mean or cruel souls, the two of you just won't connect. The people who you have shared love and life with, your loving family and friends will surely be with you when you have passed over, what springs to mind is another funny earthly saying, birds of a feather flock together, and so they do. We find it so hard to watch from the wings while you perform your play, we prompt when you forget your lines and we try to point out the mark you should be standing on so the spot light can shine upon you, and illuminate you in all your glory, and we are the ones who will give you the biggest round of applause when the scene has gone well. It's so easy for us to watch from here but just as you forget your mark and lines sometimes, we do also if or when we decide to give it another go to progress, and hopefully receive that Oscar award for a brilliant performance. So please take heart and do not fear death for it is a beautiful moment once the fear has subsided, it's a transition into another existence just the same as birth, your loved ones will be there to greet you once you have travelled through the tunnel and into the light, exactly the same experience, because it is a birth, into a new time and space. Once you have returned home with your loving family you will find it's just as hard to leave this wonderful existence and once again dwell in the world of matter.

Thank-you Father Benedict.

The Bee Hives

As I link with Father Benedict, we find ourselves on the other side of the walled garden in the meadow where the bee hives are kept, they don't look like the bee hives I'm familiar with, these are woven and look like baskets, some are hanging from the trees and some bigger ones are standing on the ground. It's a beautiful meadow full of flowers and it makes me feel so good to be here amongst nature. I wonder what we'll talk about today.

The Astral Level
This is the place where time and space have no meaning. There are many layers that make up the astral planes, and it can be said that the imagination exists here, as this is where psychic connections are made. The imagination is not something that's made up or untrue, it is what is seen in the minds-eye when an earth dweller "sees" into other dimensions like the astral plane. It is a place of knowing, and these thoughts and insights are pure imagination. It is also the first place a soul goes to after it leaves the physical body, and it's here that connections can be made. A lot of folks think it's fanciful or wishful thinking when they "see" their loved ones here, but it certainly is not, if only people could or would surrender themselves to the experience, but most are fearful of things that have no rational explanation and this is where the majority fall down or lose out, visual life is but a small part of actual life, you could find enrichment and the answers to your own, oh so many questions and problems. People look in the wrong places for their connections and answers, when it is there all the time hiding in plain sight right inside themselves.

Thank-you Father Benedict.

Rainfall

Today we are out in the field walking back towards the monastery, there is a fine misty rain beginning to fall. It's not unpleasant because it's been a hot and humid day.

I have a question for Father Benedict: Have people always used other methods of transport to make a connection with the spirit world?

Answer: By other methods do you mean alcohol, drugs and herbs? Yes. Shaman and indigenous peoples know the secrets of nature that can help to bring them the connections and answers they look for.

The natives will smoke the pipe of peace which helps to bring a calmness over arguments and disagreements because it joins spirit to spirit the people involved, and yes modern drugs and alcohol can at first take you to another place where your cares and worries seem a lot less, but these methods will only work to a certain degree because they then leave you dependent upon them and you don't seek to find personal ways to achieve peace or fulfilment. It is within everyone's reach, to find connections and healing for the mind body and spirit, ones that do not have harmful side effects but unfortunately, they do require discipline hard work and a real desire for connections via meditation and prayer. No man is an island and even if they don't always agree outwardly, inwardly everyone is seeking a connection and love with another, you all want and need emotional harmony, a sense of belonging and most of all love, because that is the very purpose of your coming into the world of matter, to seek it and to spread it.

So other methods of transport for a soul or spiritual connection are used often but for a deeper and lasting connection to take place, look within and not without.

Thank you, Father Benedict

Starlight

When Father Benedict and I connect this time, the sky is clear and full of stars and the air is fresh and crisp, the world around us is quiet and still, as we stroll along the shore. The tiny white topped waves seem to stand out in the light of the moon.

Grief

All past life incarnations are wiped clean along with the lessons learnt on the earth plane and all beneficial for growth. One very important lesson is grief which does not exist in the spirit world but plays a large part in earth life. Grief over "losing" a loved one is very real and very raw when it happens to you and it's something that needs a great deal of courage to endure. What people who are in the middle of their grief seem to forget is that everyone will grieve in their own way and in their own time, there are no guidelines to adhere to, some think after a few weeks or months I should be moving along with my life now, people will think I'm weak for breaking down so easily, but we say it will take as long as it takes. You must realise that you will never be the same person you were before, and you will be forever changed. Of course, you will! Before you were a wife or husband or son or daughter and now you are no longer in that role, so in the physical sense you are not the person you once were, but on an emotional level you may feel even closer to your loved one than you did before, and this only increases your feelings of separation.

Try to realise that separation is a physical occurrence because emotionally you can never be separated from the people you love, and who love you. In fact, in the larger picture there is no separation at all, it may look like bodies are separate which of course they are, but look more closely and you will see that every single person is part of every other single person, what they feel you feel, what you do effects what they do, no separation, but that doesn't help the grieving soul who cannot for the moment see past their loss. If the more aware of you could talk to those who haven't yet realised this and give gentle guidance and explanations it would help so much, unfortunately many are not ready to hear this as they can't see past their grief as their pain is so great. They may feel guilt for their thoughts of anger at the person who left them or anger towards themselves because their loved one was in a lot of pain and this was a blessed release for them and in this state, they can't even remember any of the good times they shared. We say do not be so hard on yourselves, your tears and sadness are a testimony to the love you shared, and all these emotions need to be worked through with time and patience. As each emotion comes to the surface deal with in the best way you can, well-meaning friends and family will say please don't cry, and give you advice but ultimately you must listen to your own heart and take your own time to come to your own conclusions. When the time is right, and things have settled down somewhat your departed loved one will try their best to make a contact with you for they are missing you as much as you are missing them, unfortunately earth people look for earth signs so they will either miss them altogether or dismiss them as wishful thinking. You need to be open-minded to all forms of communication especially anything that's personal between the two of you, listen out for songs on the radio that include words that you need to hear, it might not be "your song" or even one that you've heard before, but the words will just hit you and you will know that it has come straight from that person. You may over hear a conversation, for example, two people were discussing a friend who has gone on holiday, and one says have you heard from Jim, did he get there okay? And that was the name of your dearly departed, the answer was yes he arrived safe and sound, and this will be just the message you needed to hear, brought not from Jim himself as he wouldn't be ready yet, but from another energy source who we call an enabler, someone who has used their own energy because they will have been passed longer so therefore they are stronger, to get Jim's message to his loved one, this method is used often so please never dismiss it as wishful thinking on your part. Feathers are another lovely way for your loved one to let you know they are near, the more cynical of you may say it's only a feather and there are lots of birds around so lots of feathers too, and of course this is true but we have to use everything that's available to us, so how do you explain the ones indoors that appear from nowhere just as you were talking or thinking about them, you can't so don't even try, just take their love and know for sure they are only ever a thought away. Never be surprised if your pet or young child seems to be watching something you can't see, their awareness is on a much higher level than yours and they will recognise their family's energy straight away. Lights may flicker, doorbells may ring, televisions may turn themselves up or down or even on or off, who knows what form it will take, so don't be stuck on any idea of your own, each form of communication will be different and unique. Perhaps you will smell a familiar fragrance or cigarette smoke that no one else in the room can, that's ok it wasn't meant for them, trust your instincts and your first thoughts, they don't lie, and talk to your loved one, tell them how grateful you are for this sign and all the energy it has taken to do so, let them know their love has come through to you because if this is the first time for them to try to communicate, they won't always be sure you have understood. It takes time , lots of tears and sadness before you can begin to heal and come to accept the change that's happened to you both, it can take months or even years before you can think of them with a smile and no tears, and at special occasions like Christmas and birthdays theirs and yours, the tears will be back in full force, but as each year passes and your understanding of how life works there will be more smiles than tears and please be aware there are no time or rules for grief.

Thank-you Father Benedict. That was a very powerful message and one that I'm sure will help a lot of people.

P = Being Positive, Protected, Patient, Being Present – Living in the Now

When I started searching for my answers many years ago in church, one of the first things I saw in my minds-eye during a meditation was the letter P, I saw it clearly, entwined with green leaves and red ribbon on a parchment paper, very fancy and ornate, it was at the start of a sentence and the word was peace, the letter looked like it had been written a long time ago, it had obviously taken someone a long time to do and was drawn with loving care. I have seen it a few times since in meditation, and recently a friend of mine gave me a book about the Lindisfarne Gospels, and there at the start of one of the sentences was my letter P. Amazing! Just how I had imagined it. Instead of writing the P on my hand I now have it tattooed on my left hand just above my thumb, where I can see it constantly and it reminds me to be positive, to be in the present, and to know that I'm always safe and protected. I asked the tattooist for a letter P and she chose the style, which funnily enough turned out to be almost the same in style as my letter P. As we have said many times before there is no such thing as coincidence.

Today I am standing on the shore on the opposite side to the island, the sky is blue, and the sea is a lovely reflection of it, the sun feels warm on my back. It's the sort of day not to rush but to stand perfectly still and take in all the beauty that lies before me.

Higher Consciousness
If you require something from a partner as part of your learning experience in this lifetime, for example your soul cries out for physical touch, a child, affection, a true connection, or whatever the lesson may be, you will quite obviously be upset if it's not happening, but sometimes the very fact that you aren't experiencing it, is experience in itself. You know what you desperately need but unknown to you the lesson you require is on

a deeper level altogether. Can you go beyond the obvious and accept that they cannot give this to you because it is at this time beyond their capabilities, you could leave and miss lessons on both sides or stay with a raised consciousness and try to learn the lessons from a different perspective. Perhaps their lesson needs be learnt first, maybe they need to learn to be affectionate and tactile or expressive with their words, maybe they need to learn what a true connection really feels like, or is their lesson to be more open minded, to have a family via a different approach, do they need to think outside of their own personal box, or do you need to become aware that for now this is all they can give.

Perhaps the child you so desperately need to fulfil your maternal longings is not a biological child. You have so much love to give that you are being tested to share it with a child that's not your bloodline, but a child who has already been through so many lessons of their own. Maybe the affection you crave is there but is given in a different way, through material possessions because this is your partners way of expressing their love, whatever the reasons for these lessons, a higher consciousness is required to gain knowledge, wisdom, acceptance and an abundance of love for everyone concerned.

Thank-you Father Benedict

Saying Sorry

If you need to say sorry to anyone concerning something from the past it's never too late, if the situation allows for it, say sorry face to face but if it's going to prove detrimental to the relationship you find yourselves in now you can do it soul to soul. This is not a coward's way out and it may just be a kinder option for the other people involved, as it may well stir up too many painful memories for them but still you need to make your peace. Soul to soul is just as effective providing it's said with sincerity and love, but if you're doing it just to ease your conscience then instead of something good you will be storing up some negative karma for yourself. There are two ways to go about releasing pain, you can in your mind imagine the person in front of you and speak your words just as you would if they were there, or write down what you need to say, read it aloud, burn it and watch the smoke as it's carried to the universe to be dealt with on a higher level.

If you are immature in age or soul you won't have life's experiences to guide you, but as you grow and progress both in terms of maturity and advancement, you will realise that everyone is operating with the experiences they have. Circumstances do affect the way your life flows but as you mature, wisdom will dictate how you deal with these things. Being hurt, expecting a different reaction from people, with-holding love from each other are all the ego's work, no one is operating from hate, everyone is coming from their own idea of love and fair play, but through their own personal experiences of love they are bound to be different to yours. People have commented countless times "I just don't understand them" or where are they coming from?" and this is so easy to do when you observe situations that do not affect you directly or emotionally, but when you find yourself in the thick of it you can't see the wood for the trees. Every single person without exception is looking for their own version of love, and it's so hard when you can clearly see two people who started out so eager for life's adventures, and so in love who now just don't see eye to eye, or even understand each other at all. Everyone will grow and mature spiritually at different rates, so the people you were then are not the people you are now. More communication is needed, speaking, listening and hearing, non-judgement is needed, understanding the ego is needed and above all love is needed. It's sad to see people hurt each other with their thoughts, words and actions because there is nothing, no event or circumstance that does not have love at its centre. Everyone needs to feel special, appreciated and noticed if not, little by little their soul begins to die, to see only the negative or to point out bad things or worse still to be indifferent, which is so hurtful can cause so much harm. No- body can live a completely happy life if there is no love in it, for love is what makes the world go along in harmony, but content yourself with the sure knowledge that when you return home again all the love, support and caring you need will be yours once again.

Thank-you Father Benedict.

A Cat and Kittens

Today I find myself inside the barn sat on a bale of hay, watching a Mother cat feeding and grooming her kittens with such love and tenderness. Life is precious.

Write Your Own Story

As you get towards the end of a lifetime you can sometimes be very hard on yourself for some of the choices you made far back in your past. You start out with so much optimism and excitement for the future, and you believe that the carefree days of childhood will continue into adulthood, which of course realistically they can't because being an adult requires responsibility for yourself, and the people around you. Care-free days of youth are now replaced by care-ing days of the adult, but this doesn't have to mean it's any less fun because life is however you perceive it to be, you are the maker of your dreams and you hold the pen to write your own story, although few people realise this. It is no good waiting for life to come to you, you have to go out and grab every opportunity firmly with both hands, and mould it the way you want it, and later if it didn't turn out exactly the way you thought it would it doesn't matter, because nothing is ever a waste of time as everything adds to your knowledge and then wisdom within your spiritual growth. If you do look back and feel regret as everyone does sometimes, be assured that these were the correct decisions for the lessons you needed this time, it's never about the biggest or the best, it's about how you dealt with and are still dealing with all the little things. Look for the good within each encounter and situation you found yourself in, there will always be some. If you continue to be disappointed with yourself and your lot nothing can or will ever change, accept it, put it down and move along. You could sit around and feel sorry for yourself, and actually this is quite a good place to start from, because you are acknowledging the now, the present time and where you find yourself, so give it some thought, ponder on it for a while and then put it to one side and truly leave it where it belongs in the past, clear out the old to create space for the new to enter. If you do find you are stuck for a while in the past try not to have a crutch to lean on if possible, food, drugs or alcohol will only mask your thoughts and at some point, when you come to this realisation you will have double the trouble to deal with, so do one thing at a time properly and successfully. Everyone within reason has the same set of cards dealt to them, happiness is definitely an inside job, you could have all the money in the world and still be poor, you can be in a room full of people and be lonely, your happiness depends on you and weather you're a glass half empty or half full sort of person. If you don't like what you're experiencing, and then change your mind and not necessarily your location, running away solves nothing. To all people who look at others and think I wish I had your life, relationship, money, time, possessions, and if someone could wave a magic wand and suddenly you had all you thought you needed to feel complete, I'm afraid you would only feel this way for a short time before that little bug in your brain would be off again comparing, wishing and thinking the grass was greener elsewhere, it's not, the green grass, the blue skies and the happy place is always within you, and never without. You cannot run away from yourself no matter how hard you try, change a situation without changing yourself and before long the very same problems will show their heads again, you must deal with problems in every situation, relationship and encounter, work out why and what you did to help to fuel or create the problem, no problem or disagreement is ever one sided, accept your part in all otherwise you will be reliving your own "groundhog day" for the rest of your time on earth. Instead of asking for your life to be better ask that you may feel happiness and contentment for the one you have now.

Thank-you Father Benedict, good advice as always.

Outside the Walled Garden

Today once again I'm walking out of the walled garden and into the little meadow behind where the hives are placed, it's early spring and the flowers are so pretty, I stand and watch the bees so busy in and out of the flowers collecting their pollen, for the delicious honey that is so beneficial for good health. I'm lost in my thoughts but when I do look around, I find myself alone, I do however have these thoughts about spring, procreation, making love and I wonder…

What's it All About?
I say: We are born, we live and then we die, but what's it really, all about? We work, we strive, we love, we try our best in all we do and yet what do we really achieve by all these things?

The answer is you are all looking for the same thing in life and that's love, to give it and to receive it, there is nothing more. Nothing exists without love or through love. It is in every breath you take and every action you make, it is within every encounter and at the centre of all. You all desperately try to find it in others, you think that love means the physical, and yet this is only a part of it, you seek to experience love through another, two bodies joined together can be a beautiful experience and one you seek to re-in-act again and again for your personal gains, but you have reasons beyond the obvious for seeking pleasure with another, the obvious include closeness, comfort and connection, these things are needed to live a happy life, but do you necessarily need them from another, surely it is within all to find these levels. Beyond the physical sensations the emotional needs are probably even greater, so set aside the physical feelings for a moment, great as they are, they cannot last forever and there comes a time when the flesh, the body, becomes incapable of these actions but the feelings of giving to another are still there. The need to connect and feel close to another person never leaves, and sometimes when the physical side does come to an end the emotional side becomes even stronger, it's then time to move the emotions up to a higher level and to try to understand the meaning of life. What is it all about, what are you really doing here, why are you given situations and people to you, and what are you to do with all these feelings? Why do you crave acceptance, belonging and connection and why do you think only the physical will give this to you? What happens when the physical road to this connection is no longer an option, where do you go from there? You will have witnessed many times people who haven't manage to come to terms with this loss and haven't moved to a higher vibration, you may find they are grumpy, bad tempered, can't see the good anymore and just not so nice to be around, on some level this is understandable because it is a big thing to come to terms with, it is the reason man exists to feel connected to their fellow man. No man is an island. If you find that you question everything and still nothing makes sense, then perhaps a journey into the self is what's needed, self- discovery and exploration, what am I here for, what have I learned through my words and actions and what makes me feel alive and exhilarated, maybe it's time for your own "search for answers" because they are personal to you and always there if you look hard enough.

Thank-you Father Benedict.

Words of Advice

Although you may wish for your children to have a happy pain-free and contented life, if you keep showing them where they are "going wrong" you will end up killing their spirit. You may have the advantage of physical age and wisdom, but you can't put an old head on young shoulders, and even if you could, until someone experiences life it won't make any sense to them. It's very hard when you see them struggling, and from your own point of view the solution is so obvious, but whatever it is, it's their lesson and not yours. You cannot protect them and if you try you only make them dependent upon you, and they will lose their way. It is the right thing to do to pass on any important information but that's where you leave it, it's their choice if they take it or not, and of course sometimes their eyes and ears might not be open enough for it to have any true meaning yet. Everyone moves at their own pace and you can't hurry anyone along, there is always a natural order to everything, maybe further on down the road they will come across the same or similar experiences and your words will come back to them, and this time they will apply them. No matter how much you want to shield your children with your love you can't. Be a gentle teacher and not an aggressive preacher. Be a loving guide and support in the background and be there if they come to you, but never be in the foreground, they know without you having to voice it you will always be there for them.

Thank-you Father Benedict

Don't Give Up on Your Dreams

- Don't settle for second best and always strive for the things you know in your heart are what you need to fulfil and enrich your life.
- Keep a positive attitude for that is the only way you will attract back to you what is rightfully yours.
- Look after number one, because if you don't you won't be able to look after numbers two or three, four or more.
- Ride the waves of life as they come with all the courage and strength you can muster and remember each little setback is just another step forward, although it may not always feel that way.
- Find your tasks and lessons, approach them wisely as soon as they appear and before you know it, they will be ticked off and gone for good.
- There will be others, different ones but just as necessary, you will never stop learning and growing.
- Keep optimistic and happy and this will speed you along.
- Never try to take something that clearly is not for you, even if you want it with all your heart, your something will appear all by itself with no help or interference from you.
- If you try to force a situation you will just keep it further from you.
- Be as happy for others as you are for yourself and this attitude will take you far.
- And love, for this is the most important thing of all to have in your hearts.

Thank-you Father Benedict.

In the Kitchen

Today I find myself in the kitchen tucked away in a corner sitting beside the fireplace, cosy and warm. I'm observing and listening but not participating during this visit, I'm not even sure if the Fathers know I'm here as they are busy with their jobs. Father Andrew and Father Michael are making bread, this feels like a pleasure and a privilege as I am slowly becoming familiar with some of the other Fathers. I feel I am meant to be here listening to their conversation and not eves-dropping, as one Father listens intently to the other while he unburdens his concerns.

Everything has a Vibration and an Energy

Both come in ways that maybe you wouldn't think of as such. If someone has a problem and comes to you for help, the biggest help you can be is someone who truly listens, doesn't say a lot but gives their undivided attention and energy. They have a need to unburden their own energy because it causes them pain, and the more aware of you will know they have been sent to you because you know, how to protect yourself from being weighed down from their emotions by grounding and bubbling yourself before you meet, and if necessary leaving the conversation for a few minutes to re-apply if things get a little tense. A lot of the time people need nothing more than to talk and let go in a calm environment, with people who they know won't judge them or just nod their heads in agreement to everything that's said, but sometimes gently suggest a different approach, one they hadn't thought of themselves because their anger and pain was clouding their view. Quite often the problem will be the same one they have encountered before but this time with different players and they won't make the connection, so a calm suggestion given with love may just be the answer they're looking for. Unfortunately, in today's world people feel it is normal to turn every small upset into a big drama, and this is reinforced by what's in the media, if it's not validated by shouting and screaming it's not a problem, but by doing this you only add more energy to the already existing problem. Try to keep things in proportion, often all that's needed

In the Kitchen

is a little space between people, so they can gather their thoughts constructively, and if they do need a kind word or an ear, listen without glazing over or interrupting, and if you can do this what a wonderful friend you will be.

Thank-you Father Benedict for I know these words are yours even though I didn't see you today. And thank you Father Andrew and Father Michael for being present at today's teaching.

Everyone Must at Some Point come to their Own Conclusions About Life

It is not some kind of reward system whereby you have done something good so you get a prize, how easy and pointless would that be, and indeed some might do good turns for the sole purpose of getting the reward instead of coming from a place of love and a wishing to help.

Not everyone will have the same values as you but providing they are coming from a place of good intention, it doesn't matter how you or anyone else receives them. Beauty as they say is in the eye of the beholder and so it is, meaning all will have their own interpretation of life and each event that happens. You may feel that you've been waiting a long time for life to happen, when in reality life has been happening but perhaps not in the way you thought it should, open your eyes a little wider and see the good in all situations and people, just because things didn't turn out the way you thought they should does not make them wrong or it a wasted experience, begin right now to be grateful for all the wonderful things in your life and you will find life takes on a whole new meaning. Life, like the people who share your personal experience will decide that if you're not grateful for the things they give to you, they will stop giving.

If you feel people don't see you or they don't get you, it shouldn't make any difference, because you see you and you get you, so recognition is yours, it doesn't have to come from the outside or in a blaze of glory, ego is a strange thing. Like attracts like, so if you need to fight for someone to notice you, you will spend a lifetime fighting, never fight for anyone or anything, the way needs to be a peaceful way, a gentle unfolding for any true or lasting happiness to be yours. Trying to drag someone or something to you will in the end just keep it further from you, the universe knows better than you what you need for the lessons and learning this time so stop your struggle and let it do its job. Be at one with nature and float on top of the water, peacefully and calmly and it will support you, but lie there kicking and screaming arms flailing, and you will certainly go under, lay back and let it be, and the answers you seek will come to you. You have chosen the events and the people to help you achieve your goals; you will have the experience and can see the consequences of your thoughts, words and actions which in turn will make you happy, angry or sad. Forgive or praise everyone involved and realise from your highest level of understanding that you are all actors in your own screenplay, and when you take your final curtain call and come off stage, no one is still angry with the bad guy, now you realise what a hero he is for choosing such a difficult role and not taking the easy option, but as you also know all parts and roles must be experienced in turn, and at some point you will also be/or have been the 'bad guy', the one who needs this particular lesson. So, do not keep yourself stuck in the role of a poor me instead choose the role of the all seeing eye, the one who sees all and says nothing, no comment or no judgement, and never think that time is slipping away and you need to hurry up or you won't fit it all in, there is no rush because whatever doesn't get done in this production will get done in the next one. Always strive for knowledge and therefore wisdom, by truly understanding that whatever is and has been occurring in your life, you have attracted to you through your own thoughts, words and actions.

Thank-you Father Benedict.

Questions

Today I have two important questions for Father Benedict, about things that are affecting many people and their families on earth at this moment, particularly young adults who feel that for them there is no other option than to end their lives.

So I ask my question: Why do so many young people feel the need to return home at this time, there is so much sadness and unanswered questions for the families left behind?

Answer: It is true the universe is calling for higher and more evolved souls to return home, which is heart-breaking for the loved ones they leave behind. While on earth these poor souls feel so out of step with the world in which they find themselves, they try and try to fit in but the earth's vibrations at this time do not match theirs, and all that's happening on earth just confuses them even more until they feel powerless to halt their thoughts.

Big changes need to take place, people need to simplify their busy lives once again, earth life can become so complicated and it doesn't need to be, people step on the treadmill at the start of the day and don't look up again until they step off at night. Far too much pressure. In a lot of cases the ego is involved, there is such competition to look the best, be the best, have the latest whatever's and it becomes overwhelming trying to fit so much in, in the space of one day, simply put neither the mind or the body can cope with such demands. On some unconscious level these young people know that all this materialistic nonsense makes no-sense at all and they are pulled between trying to fit in and trying to be true to themselves. You can have all the "stuff" in the world, but it will never make up for that which they are really seeking, which is love. Friends, partners and family will all argue but we did give them love, we gave them our time and attention, but I'm afraid the love and connection they are unconsciously looking for can only be found in the world of spirit. It is so hard to understand with earth ears and eyes and you will never fully comprehend any of this while you dwell on the earth plane, but once home again contentment, connection and peace will be yours. Some may find themselves heading along that pathway and then by a turn of events veer off to the left or the right, and for a while thoughts of home are forgotten, this is because it is not yet their time, no one can or will exit before their time, it will be because their presence is still be needed upon the earth for a while to help yet to guide and to share their knowledge, and raise earths vibrations to a higher level and therefore a more compatible and peaceful place for everyone to live in.

Thank-you Father Benedict.

My Next Question

To take another life is obviously wrong, and will undoubtedly store bad karma for yourself in either this life or the next, but the question I would like to ask please is this: Is it the same if one ends one's own life?

The answer is very complex, a person will be in a great deal of torment to consider this action, some say it's a coward's way out, and some say it's very brave. Some say the mind has gone while others say the mind is very clear about what it wants. Some ask about the family that is left behind. I say nothing is ever given that one cannot cope with or have unconsciously agreed to, unfortunately most people only see with earth eyes because they are quite obviously in physical form. A life of unhappiness and torment is a hard lesson, and one that will have been thought about with much depth by an older more experienced soul before they returned to earth life, other things also come into play, personal and family karma, soul groups and family tribes, these will sometimes be seen on earth as family habits or history repeating itself, when in truth each member of the tribe will be experiencing the same lessons when they are then released as complete. When a person has reached the decision that physical life must end it is because they know the life lessons and task's they've had thus far, has led them to this point and they now recognise there does indeed have to be more meaning to life than this, and as they can remember unconsciously the love, they seek can only be found on returning home.

It has been commented more than once that people in this position will not have been in a clear state of mind and in most cases this is true, they will have had some kind of substance abuse, but that is the very reason people take these things, to be able to briefly return home, the substance's will give a sense of escaping the body and returning to where they belong and feel safe.

There is never a time that's too soon for any passing, it may feel like it to those left behind, friends and family will always question, did I do too much or not enough, but in truth you could not have changed anyone's plans, as each will have written their blueprint before leaving home. There will always be forks in the road and you may deviate onto another pathway for a while, meaning life will change and you have different experiences, but the time of passing will remain the same, no one ever returns home before their time. For the loved ones who are left behind, its very hard to come to terms with their grief and loss, and for the departed also, who will stand and observe them in tears and sometimes desperation, they so want to reach out and hug them and say: "I'm fine now. Really I am. Please do not be sad for me because I am happy and free from my earthly troubles and it is you, who I am sad for, please know without a doubt that we will be together again later, of that I can promise you."

So, does taking one's own life create negative karma for the individual? The answer is no. It takes great courage to write oneself a script like that, to inflict pain and suffering on the people you love the most, and as we have discussed before all will be recognised, peace and harmony will be with everyone when you leave the stage for the final time.

Thank-you Father Benedict I'm sure your words of wisdom will be of great comfort to many people.

On the Shore

I find myself with Father Benedict sitting on the shore. The sky is dark but lit with millions of golden stars. It's a warm calm evening and as the waves move gently in and out, they put me in an, hypnotic state, we gaze into the night sky and I'm lost in its beauty. It's then I have thoughts of my Gatekeeper John, when I feel his presence I feel safe because I know I have his protection at all times, I am so grateful to have two such wonderful helpers, one to give information and loving guidance to myself and others, to help us all to achieve an easier passage through life and the other for his love and protection. I feel I don't always give the thanks and respect that I should, so I hear and now say thank you to you both for your love, support and guidance. This journey has brought me a long way in knowledge and wisdom which I know I must pass onto anyone who needs or wants to hear it. So much has happened in the fourteen years since Dads passing, I realise it's something that I will never get over because it has changed me forever, but I now also know that it is something I have come to terms with, and I look forward with love to the day when I can be with my dear Mum, Dad and family again. I realise parting from my earth family will be so very hard for us all, but I also know without any doubt, that it's only temporary and one day we will all be together again.

I thank you both Gatekeeper John for your protection and Father Benedict for your knowledge.

Thinking Differently

My whole way of thinking is so different from back then, I can now see and understand the world and all the experiences that have shaped me and brought me to where I am now. My eyes have really been opened and for that I will be forever grateful. Life is not a power struggle or a competition (although I still have to remind myself of these facts sometimes) I don't need material possessions, I don't think I ever did I wasn't brought up that way, but things still come along and derail me from time to time and turn me into someone I'm not, but I think I understand myself and those around me better than at any other time. For life to be happy and contented it has to be peaceful, nothing will ever be found on the outside because the answers are always to be found within, it is absolutely right to question everything, but realisation has to be a personal thing to make any sense of it all, others can guide you but no one can tell you or show you.

Our thoughts are halted as we again listen to the waves and get lost in the magnificence of the sky.

Cosmic Energy

The cosmic force that binds everyone to everything lies deep inside us all, it's as far as you could travel, as near as every thought and as high as your imagination will let you go, the only thing that makes it feel complicated, vast and unfathomable is you, because you limit yourself with your thoughts. Cosmic energy is so compact that you can hold it in one hand and so vast it stretches to infinity. The energy is there for everyone to claim. It's abundant and can never get used up because it just is. Nothing is stationary, everything is in perpetual motion and the key to progression is change and acceptance, what may have seemed strange yesterday will be a perfect fit today provided you keep your heart and mind open, life will flow. Cosmic energy although unseen is swirling and moving around everything making it feel different yet comfortable, people and situations will be constantly changing as they are compatible with your own energy patterns, and once they don't fit any more it means that the two of you have unconsciously understood the work between you is complete. If the energy feels stale that means you are refusing to let go, and are holding onto something that you no longer need. As your perception of life, people and everything connected to it grows so will your relationships, the struggles of youth whether physically or emotionally begin to change and mature as you move ever forward.

Thank-you Father Benedict.

Sharing a Meal

Today I find myself in the dining hall with the Fathers sharing a meal. They sit as a family.

Family Time

They understand as do I that sharing time together around the dinner table is essential for loving growth. Sharing love and guidance with each other where everyone is both teacher and pupil is essential, you never stop learning and your quest for knowledge should never end. As people become older there is a danger of sitting back and letting go of life, but this will bring stagnation, once you stop or lose your zest for life what is there left? A standing still, a halt in advancement, a giving up and thinking this is just old age, but it doesn't have to be like this, the tables may have turned somewhat, and the children now teach the parents modern ways but that renews your zest for life. The mind is like every other muscle in the body, keep it flexible and use it regularly and it will go on and on. Your mind and body are a gift to your spirit enabling it to experience earth life with all its twists and turns, so for as long as you are a guest you might as well enjoy it to the full.

Let your children and grandchildren teach you new ways and new skills, and you in return can give them knowledge which then becomes their wisdom as they experience life in their own way. Never stop investigating or finding new ways to improve the quality of your life, and when you have new information share it with those who are ready and willing to listen, so they too may have a happy and healthy life.

Thank-you dear Father Benedict.

Life is Simple Here

Father Benedict shares this with me.

We expect nothing, and we are grateful for all that comes our way. We have no competition here, no one is trying to be better than their neighbour that would be a pointless exercise for everyone is created equal and each is on their own journey. The more we can all help each other to develop and grow, the more awareness you will achieve for yourself, because as you help others you too will grow. A life of service no matter how great or small is something to be proud of and every act of genuine kindness pays dividends to the soul, which shows itself as contentment and peace. We all seek love and happiness and that comes from within, if the inner child is happy, at peace and full of love so will the outer child be also. The truth is it comes from within and then without but so many try to practice their lives the other way around, first you find your contentment and then everything else falls into place, it just cannot happen any other way, if you are not at peace you will bring to you people and situations that are also not peaceful. As above so below, as within so without, as in heaven so on earth.

Thank-you Father Benedict.

Everyone Has the Same Opportunities

You may disagree and say how can a person who has a grand lifestyle with money to spend on all the materialistic things their hearts desire, be equal to a person who is sleeping on the streets cold and hungry, but in the eyes of spirit they are. All have free will and wherever you find yourself now is either something you needed to experience or a direct result of your past thoughts, words and actions, and this for most people is very hard to accept. Whatever you choose to do in everyday life will have a bearing on how your life shapes up. The rich man may have got his riches through hard work or good fortune but here is where the road forks, there are so many diversions to his path, he could be wealthy in terms of money and possessions but poor in terms of a loving family and friends. He could choose to put all his energy into creating a huge bank account which perhaps will give him much pleasure as he sits and looks at the figures on the paper, and if he is pleased with the way his life is going, if he doesn't need real people in his life to share his good fortune, if he is content with a life of relative solitude and doesn't require physical or emotional love because this is his point on his pathway, then he is, happy, content and fulfilled.

Another example is a different man with material wealth, he may be a humble man, quiet and kind who behind the scenes gives large sums of money to help his fellow man on the streets, or to animal shelters, or to fund medical research, so he too will feel fulfilled and peaceful because part of his journey is to share and serve, and he has taught his family to do the same, this man has used his talents and gifts to help those who are not yet at his stage of enlightenment.

Another so called wealthy man may be very clever with a quick mind, making lots of money from his business ventures and ideas, but be a cold, uncaring or unseeing man who closes his eyes to the suffering of others, his life is unfulfilled, unhappy and miserable and he doesn't understand why. So, in fact all of mankind is created equal and all of you will be presented with countless opportunities to advance, stay where you are or even move backward.

Every circumstance is unique and different, the homeless man may be on the streets because he had his wealth but stood on the heads of others to get where he was, nothing gotten in the wrong way will last. Crash! and he has lost it all, at first he complained about how unfair his life was, but after a period of time he began to think clearly, and this was all he could do, think, because now he had nothing else to fill his time with, he began to realise that he had been unfair in his dealings and so became excepting of his circumstances, and actually started to look out for other people on the streets who were in a worse state than himself, this gave him the love peace and fulfilment he had never had in his former life. It's never too late to change, everyone is created equal with the same opportunities for growth no matter what their surroundings or circumstances, it's therefore up to the individual if they take the opportunity or not.

Thank-you Father Benedict, lovely words.

Outside the Barn

Today when I link in with my Guide and dear friend Father Benedict, we find ourselves sitting on small wooden stools outside the barn, there are reeds scattered all around and once more we are basket weaving, this is something I enjoy as I am very practical and like to make things especially from natural materials. We sit in comfortable silence as we work.

Thought Bubbles

It is just as important to keep your thoughts positive and pure as it is to keep the spoken word the same. Your spoken words convey to the world your attitude and beliefs, but to some extent you modify them to suit the company you find yourself in, sometimes out of politeness, sometimes out of concern for their feelings and sometimes because of your ego, you wish to appear better, kinder or more considerate than you really are. Your thoughts are a whole different matter; you may say one thing but think something completely different. Wouldn't it be strange if above everyone's head there was a thought bubble, just like the ones that appear in the comic books, and how strange if everyone could read the true thoughts of others. How upsetting that might be. In reality of course there is no thought bubble but on some level of understanding, and at some point later when you, yourself do your own life review you will as everyone will, be able to see the thoughts and opinions of others and how your own thoughts and opinions have affected them, and they you, so maybe a thought bubble would actually be a good way to keep those unhelpful or unhappy thoughts at bay. If every thought, you ever had about everyone was in plain sight you would try so hard to keep them positive and pure. Of course, you can't agree with everyone about everything and it's very healthy to have your own opinion but that's where you would leave it because no one really wants to hurt another's feelings all because they couldn't control their thoughts.

Thank-you Father Benedict.

Use Your Senses

When you are born into the world of matter all thoughts of past lives get wiped from your mind, each time is like the first time and it is your job to see how far you can progress from the knowledge that comes your way. You all have the gift of intuition and can pick up so much from every person you meet. You may believe that you possess five senses, but you do have six, the sixth one being that of knowing, or receiving information telepathically and you all have that to some degree.

In past times, it was relied upon a lot, today not so much, which is a shame because it is a very useful tool to have, if you listen to what's commonly known as your gut feeling it can save you from a lot of heartache or give you a lot of joy. You will be receiving messages via your intuition all the time, but you will dismiss them as wishful thinking or fearful thinking but try if you can to become aware of them once again because as with all gifts, the more you use them the stronger, they become. In the past there were no weather reports on the television, people would go outside and "feel" the air around them, look at the sky, stand and absorb the atmosphere and know or at least have a fair idea of what the weather would be doing, who does that today, probably only the farmers because are still in touch with nature. They can sense when one of their animals is not well because they are in tune with their own vibrations and those of their animals.

There are so many ways to communicate without using words, body language or facial expressions are a good indicator, people often say they are fine when they aren't, learn to look into their eyes because you can tell so much from them, they are not called the windows of the soul without good reason, they will be giving the true answers not the tongue. Listen to your gut it speaks the truth, but most people are just too busy to hear, listen to your body it's talking to you all the time, that little twinge of pain is letting you know it needs rest as well as play, take heed and do something about it before it becomes more serious. Listen to those pangs of guilt when you've made an inappropriate comment or hurt someone's feelings, an apology goes along way.

Use your Senses

Watch your children closely and tune into their moods, they might be too young to know themselves when things are not as they should be, perhaps something is amiss at school and they don't tell you but their body language will, dropped shoulders, an unhappy face or just standing a little too close to you for their comfort and reassurance, use your intuition, you can't always make the problem disappear but you can make it easier for them to open up and talk about it. Learn to listen to what people aren't saying rather than what they are, learn to shut off your own mind chatter because gifts are given so you may use them.

Thank-you Father Benedict.

Early Morning

As we link together in the early morning, I find Father Benedict sweeping the cloisters, which is the covered walkway that connect the buildings of the monastery, he uses a broom made from twigs, further along I see Father Thomas doing the same.

Confidence and Change

To move forward with one's life, you should attempt to do so with a calm confidence; it's quite alright if you don't have a clear picture of where you are headed provided you have the confidence to move. To move and change is what living is all about, never be afraid of change for change is growth, do not cling to old out- dated ideas and values just because they are comfortable, strive and stretch yourself and be open to a new way of looking at your life, sweep out the old and in with the new. If you have constantly viewed your life in a certain way and now feel stuck and unmotivated you must change to a new pattern of thought. New people and situations will then be presented to you by the very nature of your new thoughts and you can be part of an exciting new way of living your life, if people didn't accept change or a different way of thinking everyone would still believe the world was flat, and if you strayed too far you would fall off the edge. The one thing that limits you and therefore keeps you stuck is your own mind, just because something is new to you it doesn't mean it won't work, new ways of looking at the same old problems can be fresh and exciting, your scientist may consider the task one hundred times and still come up with the same results, but approaching it with a slightly different point of view will give the information they require a chance to filter through from a new angle. There is an answer to every question no matter how big or small provided you are open to the possibilities, don't continue to go around in circles, open your eyes, hearts and minds and hear instead of just listening to what's being said, consider the un-thinkable. Trust your own judgement for no one knows you better than you, surprise someone as well as yourself with your newfound spontaneity, and watch how your new life unfolds.

Thank-you Father Benedict.

Moving Forward

When you recognise the reason behind all actions can accept them without judgment and "know" this is the way it is, can you really move forward to peace. Only when you leave all longings, dissatisfaction and envy behind, will you finally know contentment. This is the path and the knowledge, the life and lessons you chose to experience, so give up the fight and let things run their natural course, no one tells the river which way to flow, it 'knows', and when it follows its natural course it can even cut through rock with no effort at all. Life doesn't always happen in the way you think it should, expectations just let you down so don't hold on to them, be open to change and go with the flow of life instead of against it. Nothing is permanent, everything changes, and this is the natural order. Your life is as good as you believe it to be, if you start to acknowledge this you will open the way for more good things to come to you, but when you close your eyes to it all you put a block on letting any good come to you. A lot of people can talk the talk, but they have trouble walking the walk. It's easy to see where others are going wrong but when things are right under your nose it's hard to see it. When you can begin to recognise your patterns this is when you are beginning to move forward, and you'll know this by the way you feel, light and somewhat excited but you won't necessarily know why, it may be like the feeling of having a secret or waiting for a special treat, the trick is to keep this feeling alive, add to it, acknowledge everything in your life that gives you pleasure and reasons to smile, and when in this happy frame of mind you will attract the perfect people and situations to help you further along, hold no expectations or have no set ideas as to how it will turn out just stay open, happy and grateful.

Thank-you Father Benedict.

Look After Yourself

Time spent alone is some of the most important time you can create, peaceful time where you are not thinking of anything. The stillness of your mind creates space for new ideas to come into your reality and be born. Being alone, sitting quietly and allowing yourself to rest physically, emotionally and mentally will give you an increasingly clear sense of self, because it's in these still times where you are not playing out any role or identity, that your soul or higher consciousness can speak clearly to you. You have a distinct sense of your own energy when others are not around. Some of you are with other people so much of the time that when you do finally find yourself alone it feels strange, so you then create a list of things you must do, anything to keep from thinking and reflecting on your life. You have been taught that being busy and productive, creating things that you can touch and see is what counts, however reflective time is the source of energy revitalisation, of clear seeing, of ideas, inspiration and spiritual contact. Start to value any alone time where you can sit and just be, for stillness is the doorway to sensing and opening your intuition, also the highest and most effective form of self-healing.

Thank-you Father Benedict.

Closing

When I get into my quiet space, this time I find myself on the shore in the moonlight, the sky is filled with hundreds of twinkling stars. The causeway is open and it's very quiet as I walk away from the island, the only sound I hear is the sea lapping quietly and gently in and out on either side of me. Once I'm on the other side I sit on the sand and look back across to our island, Lindisfarne, Holy island, the special place in my heart where so many of my questions have been answered, where I have been privileged to meet and make good friends of my Gatekeeper John, Father Benedict and the other Fathers and Brothers. Amid the hustle and bustle of life it's so nice to just sit and be, to take time out and enjoy the present moment. It has been said that the past has gone, the future is yet to come, and the present is a gift, so enjoy it. I sit on the sand and look upwards to the sky, once more I feel myself float up into the calm, midnight blue. There are so many questions I would like to ask.

How do I know if I'm following my path? Is this my chosen mission? How do I know if my random thoughts are correct and should I trust them? Should I try to push myself in the direction I feel is right, or should I sit back and do nothing while waiting for my destiny to find me? It's easy to hear the words trust yourself you will know what's right, but will I?

One of the hardest things to accomplish is trust in oneself and the universe, but until you can do so and let go you will be forever doubtful. Some of the time you will get it wrong, but mistakes are there to be learnt from, and honestly nothing is ever that bad that you can't put it right to some degree, and at least you will have taken that leap of faith and won't be standing still, wondering to yourself, what if? If you really are at a crossroads and don't know which way to go, sit right down and do nothing, take a breath and ask for a sign, you won't be disappointed. Sometimes you may feel you are ready to handle something and wonder why it's taking so long to materialise, you get frustrated and angry at the delays, but maybe they are there for a reason, you feel ready but the universe doesn't agree, maybe there are still a few loose ends to tie, there will be many reasons just go with the flow of things and let the universe do its job. Know that no one or nothing can disturb your peace of mind unless you allow it. A wise person will rise above harsh words or action or remove themselves. Give everyone the benefit of the doubt, try to be fair and the most important thing of all is to love, to feel it and to give it, to teach it and to be it. To try to be the best person you can be without compromising yourself in any way, self-love is as important as loving another. Love is all there is, all that has ever been, and all there will ever be.

Thank-you Father Benedict.

And thank you for taking the time to read these teachings, and if they have spoken to you please pass on to others what you have learned.

Thank You.